Reclaiming the Fire

Reclaiming the Fire

Depth Psychology in Teacher Renewal

Clifford Mayes, Mark R. Grandstaff, and Alexandra Fidyk

ROWMAN & LITTLEFIELD
Lanham • Boulder • New York • London

Published by Rowman & Littlefield
An imprint of The Rowman & Littlefield Publishing Group, Inc.
4501 Forbes Boulevard, Suite 200, Lanham, Maryland 20706
www.rowman.com

6 Tinworth Street, London SE11 5AL, United Kingdom

British Library Cataloguing in Publication Information Available

Library of Congress Cataloging-in-Publication Data Available

ISBN: 978-1-4758-1369-2 (cloth : alk. paper)
ISBN: 978-1-4758-1370-8 (pbk. : alk. paper)
ISBN: 978-1-4758-1371-5 (electronic)

♾️™ The paper used in this publication meets the minimum requirements of American National Standard for Information Sciences—Permanence of Paper for Printed Library Materials, ANSI/NISO Z39.48–1992.

Contents

Introduction

Foundations of the Teacher's Sense of Calling

We have written this book in the belief that most teachers go into their profession out of praiseworthy, even heroic, motives. Cliff's, Mark's, and Alexandra's combined seventy years of researching why people choose the often-difficult route of teaching and their combined ninety years of teaching—one that has many emotional benefits but also many emotional demands and limited financial rewards, especially under the insensitive and uninformed requirements of policy imposing standardized curriculum and instruction—has convinced them that most teachers feel "called" to teach. Teachers tell us that this call comes from something higher or deeper, and certainly bigger, than themselves. Sometimes the calling has to do with *whom* they will teach—their love for their students. Sometimes it revolves around *what* they will teach—their passion about the subject matter. Usually it's a combination of both.

This doesn't mean that every educator is a "called teacher"—the phrase we will use to describe such teachers. Some individuals' motives are nothing out of the ordinary and would certainly not require an entire book to understand, celebrate, and nurture. Such people take up teaching because, for example, they like being free all summer. Some teachers with families are drawn to the excellent benefits that the job may provide if they are working for the state. Some become teachers because it was a fallback position that they had cleverly kept in their rear pocket in case some "bigger" professional goal didn't pan out, and it didn't.

Still, our experience as researchers and teachers convinces us that many, perhaps most, teachers are *called* teachers. Their teaching is intimately tied into their life narratives. Because of this, one can gain insight into how and why a teacher teaches the way she does only by knowing something about her life, and one can begin to understand a called teacher's life only by considering how important teaching is in it. In other words, teaching is core to who the called teacher is as a human being. We guess that most of you who are reading this book would agree that this is true of you.

Therefore, it is to the teacher's core that we must turn our attention if we are to help that teacher define or refine her vision of herself as a teacher in ways that are emotionally, intellectually, and ethically engaging and productive.

To accomplish this, we will draw in this chapter upon five thinkers who have been important in our personal and scholarly lives. Three of them are notable psychological theorists/therapists—Heinz Kohut (1913–1981), Donald Winnicott (1896–1971), and Abraham Maslow (1908–1970). The other two are perhaps the most influential Existentialist theologians of the twentieth century—one from the Jewish tradition named Martin Buber (1878–1965) and the other from the Christian tradition named Paul Tillich (1886–1975).

After looking at these five highly influential people in the twentieth century and employing their thoughts in chapter 1 to help us better understand and care for the teacher's sense of calling and how to nurture it, we will turn in chapter 2 to the greatest psychospiritual theorist and practitioner of them all—Carl Gustav Jung (1875–1961), who will be our main focus—although we will continue to draw upon the five figures examined in this chapter.

Although these six psychological and spiritual giants were working about a half century ago, their insights are as powerful today as they were then—perhaps even more so given the current corporate agenda to standardize education and thereby take the soul out of it. Indeed, it is precisely because we are so aware of the impossible demands placed upon teachers these days, which overtax already-valiantly devoted and terribly overworked teachers and which also continue to ignore the fact that the problems children face are not a product of our schools but of our society at large that we have written this book. Our fervent hope is that it will help you renew your noble sense of mission so that, even in these trying times for teachers, you will feel more fulfilled in all that you accomplish, will discover ways to renew your vision of yourself as a teacher despite all the grossly and unjustly negative things that are said about teachers, and will find new ways of continuing in your extremely important work. We have often turned to them in our scholarly writing. We feel that you will find these great thinkers as useful as we have over the years in how they chart out the human depths in ways that help us understand profoundly why one becomes a teacher and how to forge an ever more beautiful and empowering vision of oneself as a teacher as one moves along the developmental life path.

We will do this by painting in very broad strokes the ideas of those thinkers and how they relate to the art and craft of teaching. Accompanying that are exercises in the form of individual meditation and journal writing, dyadic conversations, group processing, and more for you to engage in based on those ideas.

PSYCHOLOGY, SPIRITUALITY, AND
THE CALLED TEACHER

Unlike Freud, the founder of psychoanalysis, the two *post-Freudian* theoreticians and psychoanalysts Heinz Kohut and Donald Winnicott felt that what basically powers the psyche is *the need for authentic relationship with others*. In their view, it is the quest for connectedness that is the driving force of the individual's psyche. The psychological models and terms they introduced will help us understand the teacher's sense of calling, which is so often rooted in the need to relate in life-shaping ways with students. It will also provide us with some clues and how to help that sense of calling grow.

Buber presents in religious terms what Kohut and Winnicott put in their own specialized vocabulary—namely, that happiness and health reside primarily in relationship.

As a theologian, however, Buber goes even further regarding the dynamics of relationship in insisting that one can't hope to have a vibrant and loving connection with the Transcendent or Divine (whatever one might conceive that to be) without being in vibrant and loving connection with others. Love of one's fellows and love of the Transcendent go hand in hand, Buber insisted. When both kinds of love exist, both of them thrive. But when one of the two great loves is absent, the other kind of love proves itself to be ultimately hollow and shaky. Buber called relationship with the Divine through others and with others through the Transcendent an *I-Thou relationship*.

On the other hand, if one is treating others merely as objects, that is an *I-It* relationship. Treating people as objects leaves a person mired in non-relationship. Living in the light of *I-Thou* relationship, said Buber, is the essence of the ethical life. The darkness of the *I-It* mode—the objectification of others—is the root of false and unethical living.

We have spent a great deal of our lives as scholars and teachers pondering and writing about the many ways in which Buber's ideas help clarify and magnify the teacher's sense of calling, for this calling necessarily involves the teacher's sense of what is profoundly good. We would like to share those ideas with you and offer suggestions about how you might use them to enrich your classroom practice.

The theologian Paul Tillich introduced a phrase that has been greatly influential in twentieth-century theology, and its educational implications and applications are many, as Cliff has discussed in other works (Mayes, 2009; Mayes, 2007). That phrase is "ultimate concern."

In a sense, no one is an atheist, said Tillich, for at the deepest core of one's life are some foundational beliefs that ethically and philosophically guide that person's life—whether or not that person is clearly aware of them, or even aware of them at all. These are the individual's "ultimate concerns," which, says Tillich, *are* more or less that person's "god," for they are what a person considers final and finally valuable, both the source and goal of value. This has been a traditional definition of God for thousands of years, at least in the monotheistic traditions.

To become ever more aware of one's "ultimate concerns," to find ways to make them grow in passion and compassion, and to live in ever greater fidelity to them—this, said Tillich, is true spirituality. Since a fair number of teachers see a spiritual side to their work, we will use Tillich's idea to help them clarify and intensify that dimension of their labor of love.

Returning to psychology, we will take up the work of Abraham Maslow (1908–1970). Although a "humanist" psychologist—a school rooted in Existentialist philosophy and not a strictly psychoanalytic one—Maslow, along with Winnicott and Kohut, nevertheless believed that the formation and care of a vibrant, empowered self was the goal of psychological development—the apex of his famous pyramidal "hierarchy of needs" model.

As his work evolved, however, Maslow came to assert that creating a healthy ego was, although necessary, not adequate in accounting for the more cosmic aspect of psyche, which feels incomplete and can even grow ill without enjoying some sort of connection with the Divine or Transcendent (again, however one conceives of divinity or transcendence).

In other words, Maslow's picture of the integral and powerful psyche was one that took account not only of the personal, ego-based features of the psyche but also those parts of psyche that instinctively needed to connect with something higher—something *trans*-personal—in order to rise to its full stature as something that was not just personal but also something transpersonal.

After examining in more depth in the following chapter all the ideas just introduced and applying them to one's calling and practices as a teacher, we will then turn in chapters 2 and 3 to the work of Carl Gustav Jung, who we believe to be the greatest transpersonal psychologist of the twentieth century and the one whose work applies most fully and forcefully to the teacher's sense of calling.

Cliff's twenty-five-year project of exploring the possibilities of Jungian psychology in this connection has resulted in ten books and forty articles in scholarly journals and led to the creation of a field of instructional theory called "Jungian pedagogy." Mark's three-decade work ranges from personally advising two presidents of the United States in the Oval Office as a high-ranking air force officer to the professorship to writing nationally celebrated books in business and leadership that draw upon these psychologists and especially upon Jung. Alexandra has been a school teacher in her native land, Canada, and is now an associate professor in teacher education at the University of Alberta. She has been a moving force in establishing and expanding Jungian educational scholarly societies and is already acknowledged as a leading figure in the field of Jung and education. Additionally, she is a poet and this plays into her work in uniquely moving ways as you will see in her concluding chapter in this book.

So without further ado, let us begin our journey into greater self-knowledge and efficacy as a teacher by encountering these great thinkers and exploring how their thoughts can expand our vision of ourselves as teachers.

Chapter One

Five Psychospiritual Thinkers of the Twentieth Century and What They Can Tell Us about the Teacher's Sense of Calling

HEINZ KOHUT

Heinz Kohut is the father of "self-psychology." According to self-psychology, the creation and maintenance of a stable and integral *self* is the primary psychological need and overarching goal. At the very of core of psyche, Kohut insisted, is the desire to become an integral person in relationship with other integral individuals. But what is meant by this phrase "an integral person"?

An integral person is one whose many different aspects, experiences, desires, fears, hopes, and needs have been acknowledged, worked with and through, and then brought together to become blended and balanced. The result of this process is what Kohut called "healthy narcissism."

Although the word "narcissism" has negative connotations in popular use, Kohut simply meant by it how a person views and values himself. If he has a realistic and generally positive estimation of himself, knows his limitations, appreciates his strengths, and is able to laugh good-naturedly at his own and others' inevitable human foibles, he has achieved a *healthy narcissism*. The person who does not live in the desired state of healthy narcissism suffers from what Kohut called a *narcissistic wound*.

The roots of a person's sense of self lie in his earliest relationships with his primary caregivers. Kohut called the persons who make up the infant's earliest relational world his *self-objects*. It is through a person's self-objects that he comes to know who he is since we know ourselves only in relationship with others. Through them the infant learns about the world and itself. The self-object is not, in the final analysis, *actually* the other person. Rather it is the feeling-toned *image* of that person that the infant—and later the adult—has internalized or, in psychoanalytic language, has *introjected* in his psychological system in early interactions with that primary "other"—or those "others."

5

Typically the infant's most influential self-object is its mother. The infant's psyche is so dramatically shaped by its interaction with its mother because it is almost totally fused with her at these first stages of its development. Indeed, in the infant's earliest experience the mother *is* the whole of reality itself to the infant, according to many developmental psychologists. The nature of the mother's—or any primary caregiver's—interaction with the child will determine the nature of the child's *primary narcissism,* whether it is healthy or not.

Thus, if the mother's interaction with the infant conveys feelings of love and acceptance, the infant learns that he is loveable and accepted and that the world is reliable and good. The infant comes to see himself as essentially a beautiful, stable, and unified being. In this way, the child's *primary narcissism* is satisfied in its communion with the loving mother. This is healthy narcissism, and it is brought about in two ways.

The first is in what Kohut called *the mirroring transference.* Transference in psychoanalytic theory and practice is how individuals exchange and interpret the emotions that flow between them. It typically involves mutual projections, which is another way of characterizing the transference. In the mirroring transference, the infant sees and defines itself through the mirror of its mother's responses to it. The infant and later child knows who he is because of his mother's response to him.

The second is in *the idealizing transference.* The infant, enshrining the mother as not only the culmination of reality but indeed *as* reality, finds its own ideals and ideal state in its merger with this god-like figure. The idealizing transference is the root of the child's ability, or inability, to form and develop a value system.

The opposite of this kind of self-esteem-creating and value-enabling mother is the one who communicates to the infant in her interactions with it that she is unhappy that it has come into the world, anxious about the infant, or even repelled by it. This lays the foundation for a variety of psychological illnesses in the developing infant that result in *the narcissistic personality disorders* in later years.

For what the infant now sees in the "mirror" of the mother is what it comes to conclude is its own ugliness, weakness, and fragmentation. The world is neither welcome nor welcoming, but rejecting, cold, perilous, and confusing: a place that is either valueless or whose values are unattainable or seem irrelevant to the child's forming mind.

The narcissistic personality disorders are distorted attempts to experience the primary mirroring and idealizing that a person never experienced as an infant—or never experienced enough. These manifestations of isolation are called *secondary narcissism.* Healthy human development originates in *healthy primary narcissism.* But when primary narcissistic needs are not met, the many problems of *unhealthy secondary narcissism* are bound to occur.

As both a theorist and therapist, Kohut was fascinated by the relationship between healthy narcissism and productivity. He explored "the ways by which a number of complex and autonomous achievements of the mature personality [are] derived from transformations of narcissism—i.e., created by the ego's capacity to tame narcissistic cathexes [releases of psychic energy] and to employ them for its highest aims" (Block, 1997; Britzman, 2011). Healthy narcissism manifests itself in creativity, compassion, wisdom, and humor.

Educational Implications and Applications of Kohut's Ideas

The uses of Kohutian self-psychology in education are many and have been developed by educational theorists who are interested in the highly charged psychodynamic energies that circulate through the classroom (Block, 1997; Britzman, 2011). Here we will touch on some of the major self-object issues in the classroom.

The first has to do with the many similarities that researchers have noted between the role of a mother and a teacher—even if the teacher is a male, for providing nurturance is not limited to women. Indeed, the connection between the maternal function and the teaching function should not be too surprising since the mother *is,* after all, the child's first teacher at both conscious and unconscious levels, and since many men as well as women come to teaching out of the noble need to build children up cognitively, emotionally, and ethically.

In how she introduces the baby to the world and what she focuses on as being significant or ignores as insignificant, in the things or people she prizes and those that she disdains, in how she interprets for the child the situations in which she and her child find themselves together, the mother is the source of the child's first and most influential "life-lessons."

As important as what she is teaching the baby about the world is what she is teaching the baby about *himself.* In the tenderness and acceptance or in the tension and rejection with which she is holding and relating to the baby, she is communicating to the child that he is good person and a good learner in an open and exciting world, or that he is a bad person and learner and that the world is a closed and disappointing, even terrifying, place. It is probable that many so-called learning disabilities stem from an early damaged relationship between the student and his mother, or whoever the primary caregiver may be.

As noted, the mother is typically the child's first *psychological self-object,* teaching the child who he is *as a person.* In a related manner it is fair to say that the child's teachers are his ongoing *pedagogical self-objects,* teaching the child who he is *as a learner.* The importance of the teacher's role becomes immediately clear when we consider that a person's general evaluation of himself is closely tied into his evaluation of himself as a learner.

A person who sees himself as a bad learner—as "stupid"—is not very prone to esteem himself very highly in any domain of his life. "What does it matter what I think or feel or do? I'm just stupid."

The connection between mothers and teachers has often been recognized and makes intuitive sense. It even shows up in the language we use to describe learning in terms of taking in food—a process associated with the mother from time immemorial. We talk about "consuming" or even "devouring" a meal just as we do a book. We must then take time to "digest" both—to "chew on things." Sometimes we wind up just "regurgitating" what we've just taken in. Other times we "savor" and really "chew on" what has been "prepared" for us and get so "filled up" with good information and ideas that we can't "take in" any more. Or we get so "fed up" with bad information and ideas that we can't "stomach it" and "could just spit."

Mothers who are good psychological self-objects for their child lay the foundation for the development of a strong ego-structure in him, one that, in healthy narcissism, can relate to others in lively curiosity, ethical clarity, and genuine compassion. In like manner, teachers who are good pedagogical self-objects help students develop what is called a strong learning ego, one that can relate not only to the teacher in a constructive way but also to new knowledge with curiosity and clarity, and in compassionate interaction with other seekers after knowledge.

We have already seen that this happens between the mother and child largely through the two types of transferences—the mirroring and the idealizing. These two transferences also take place in the classroom between the teacher and student.

In a successful mirroring transference in the classroom, the student senses his worth as a learner in the teacher's accepting eyes, her authoritative but non-aggressive body language, her constructive criticism balanced with praise, her curiosity about and faith in the student's potential, her timely and complete responses to the work he turns in, and her gentle humor. This is not a naïve faith in the teacher that every student is capable of the same levels of mastery of a skill or body of knowledge. It is simply the faith that this student standing before her is capable of more than he knows, and that his growth potential is enormous.

In the evolving mirroring transference throughout the term, the student grows increasingly confident that this teacher will stand by him in his cognitive unfolding. She will rejoice with him in his victories and also help him regroup after those stumbles and occasional falls that are an inevitable part of creative evolution. And she will gently laugh with him about not only his but also her limitations in confronting the relentless puzzles and endless depths of knowledge.

What the student sees mirrored in the teacher's trust and trustworthiness is his own possibilities, indeed his destiny, as a learner on the road to greater empowerment. This comes to pass because the teacher, a healthy pedagogical self-object, nurtures the student in the mirroring transference in the classroom.

The teacher also will ideally manage the *idealizing transference* with the same kindness and skillfulness. The primary caregiver optimally provides a model for the infant and then child to look up to, emulate, and thereby fashion a competent and caring life on. Similarly, the teacher provides an example for the student of what it means to be a responsible and courageous learner.

The teacher is an exemplar for the student to adopt and adapt to his own needs and temperament in how she explores issues with her students in class. The teacher worthy of emulation by the student appropriately (not showily!) evidences her expertise but also her eager willingness to grow in knowledge through respectful exchanges with the student, who also brings what Gonzales has called his own body of knowledge to the learning endeavor. Also through consulting other sources or searching more deeply inside herself when she does not know the answer to a question, she shows her own willingness to learn.

With such a teacher, the student catches a vision of how to be an effective and humane learner. And in how the teacher mixes both demand and care in order to strike just the right balance in her healing presence, she creates the conditions for an idealizing transference to take shape in the student.

If the teacher sees that these transferences are not taking root in the student, she may well suspect that the student is suffering from a narcissistic wound that is not allowing him to "metabolize" her positive transference onto him. This is true in many cases because the student had had little, if any, experience of such affirmation in his larger life. Indeed, the student may fear that the teacher is lying to him or "playing" him by pretending that he is a good learner when, of course, he knows very well that he is not.

In identifying a negative transference in a student, the teacher will usually not know the cause of it since she is not a therapist and therefore not privy to what in the student's life has led to this blockage and agony in him. The teacher is not a therapist, nor should she try to be.

But she can be a *therapeutically sensitive teacher* who understands the fragile and complex psychodynamics at play in the learning process—what Salzberger-Wittenberg (1989) has very correctly called "the emotional experience of teaching and learning."

The therapeutically sensitive teacher turns the space in which she teaches into a *therapeutic classroom*. The teacher accomplishes her pedagogically therapeutic role simply by caring for and believing in her student in her various interactions with him in the course of an everyday class. And it cannot be stressed enough that this occurs when the teacher mixes a high level of demand with a high level of care in her relationship with the student.

High demand with low care leads to the teaching style called "authoritarian teaching." It is too harsh, leading to either servile submission or angry resistance in the student. However, low demand with high care leads to the teaching style called "permissive," which a student may be all too happy to exploit. It coddles the student, who therefore has no reason to grow. It is the balance of high care *and* high demand that leads to the optimal teaching style—"authoritative," which, not incidentally, is also the best parenting style. Again, we see the parallels between teaching and parenting in their best therapeutic manifestations (Conger & Galambos, 1997).

If the teacher does not try to strike this balance, she turns herself into a *therapeutically insensitive teacher,* even a psychologically destructive one, whose disregard for the student's heart and mind in balance causes her to create *therapeutically insensitive classrooms*. This hinders learning—sometimes fatally forecloses it—in a classroom. Such teachers can be toxic, killing the student's joy in learning and thus betraying the teacher's calling to nurture her students in knowledge.

Finally, the teacher must attend to her own "narcissistic wounds," as must we all. Otherwise, she might well try to compensate for them by exercising her inherent power as a teacher in ways that harm her students. We have all had at least one teacher who engages in hurtful "power-trips" over students. This kind of totalitarian teaching style almost certainly stems from a teacher's narcissistic wounds, as Cliff has discussed in other work (Mayes, 2017).

In what seems to be an opposite teaching style but one that stems from the same unfulfilled need to be healthily validated, there is the teacher who simply coddles her students or tries to be "one of the gang" in order to win her students' love. The cure for both bullying by the teacher and inappropriate emotional intimacy with her students is that she reflects deeply upon how her own ego issues may be clouding her judgment and diminishing her effectiveness as a teacher. This reflectivity on the teacher's part is the first step in ensuring that she finds *her power* not in lording it over or emotionally seducing her students but rather in *empowering them*.

Exercises in Reflectivity Using Kohut's Ideas

Exercise 1: In a private journal that you keep for the purposes of this course, look back on your own caregivers[1] during your growing-up years. Did you incur "narcissistic wounds" in the mirroring and idealizing transferences that occurred between you and them? How may these wounds have played a part—however small or great—in your decision to become a teacher? How do they affect how you currently see yourself as a teacher? How might they be affecting your classroom practices in the ways in which you view and interact with certain students or with the class as a whole?

Conversely, what positive mirroring and idealizing transferences occurred in your youth, and how might they have impacted your decision to teach? What strengths have they provided in your ego-structure, and how has this contributed to your success as a teacher? How might you build upon them to become a teacher with a healthy ego-structure that helps your students develop such a structure as well, especially a strong "learning ego"?

Exercise 2: To the degree that you may feel comfortable doing so, share some of what you have written with a partner and let him help you process that part of your journey to become a teacher and your current classroom practices. Then switch roles as you listen to what he or she has to share. Can you help each other come to a deeper understanding of the issues that the other chose to share?

Exercise 3: As a class, discuss whether or not it is true that a classroom must have either a therapeutic or antitherapeutic effect? Have the authors put the case too strongly? What are possible dangers or pitfalls in trying to create a therapeutic classroom? Yet, what are possible dangers in *not* creating such a classroom "space"?

Also discuss whether it is important for you as a teacher to see that the students in your classroom not only learn what is being taught in the official curriculum but also develop strong identities as highly functioning "learning egos." Is this important to you? Why? Is it unimportant or irrelevant to you as a teacher? Why?

Exercise 4: In your journal, think back on your own experiences as a student with a teacher who provided a positive mirroring and idealizing transference. Then think back of one who inflicted negative transferences on you. How has this affected you as a learner and now a teacher over the years? Be prepared to discuss at least a few of these ruminations with a member or members of your class.

Exercise 5: Prepare a one-paragraph statement to be read in groups of four or five students about what you have essentially taken away from this discussion of Kohut's psychology and educational implications and applications.

D. W. WINNICOTT

Three of Winnicott's constructs have proven fruitful in the study of depth psychology and teaching: *holding environments*, *good-enough mothering*, and *transitional objects*.

Like Kohut, Winnicott saw the foundations of psychological health or illness in the infant's relationship with its mother. Foremost of the conditions for healthy psychological growth is that the mother provide the infant with a *good holding environment.*

This is a space in which the child feels protected—or "held"—and thus feels confident in exploring that space in stable and authentic relationship with the mother. The developing child, from the secure and attentive home base of a good holding environment, also feels capable and worthy of moving in small increments out of that safe space in order to encounter and explore other people and places just beyond the reach of his good holding environment. He has *the courage to try* (Bernstein, 1989).

The first holding environment that the mother provides for the infant is in the environment of her arms, where, in the paradise of mother's embrace, the infant is literally "held" in the nurturing environment of her bosom. From this safe space, the infant surveys its world, feels welcome in it, and is poised to move forward in that world in honesty and power.

This holding environment expands in physical, cognitive, and emotional scope as the mother creates other environments in which the infant grows in wider and wider circles of confidence and possibility. From mother's arms to the little semicircle around her chair to the playroom to the living room to the whole house and finally into the wide world that lies just beyond the front door, the child experiences existence in ever greater degrees of freedom, maturing in health.

Without good holding environments created by the caregiver for the child, the child feels exposed, vulnerable, and therefore hyperdefensive and overly strategic in his dealings with others. Without a good holding environment, the infant naturally learns to focus mostly on just surviving. Self-expression, creativity, and humane interaction with others become very rare luxuries, even irrelevancies, in the child's embattled existence, according to Winnicott.

For the child develops what Winnicott termed "the False Self," who cannot be in healthy communication with others because communication rests on authenticity. Otherwise, it is not communication but deception. Since clear and compassionate relationship with others is the primary psychological need according to the self-object psychologists, such a child has been set up from the beginning for the full spectrum of neuroses.

Winnicott goes on to state that

> a wide extension of "holding" allows this one term to describe all that a mother does in the physical care of her baby, even including putting the baby down when a moment has come for the impersonal experience of being held by suitable non-human materials. In giving consideration to these matters, it is necessary to postulate a state of the mother who is (temporarily) identified with her baby so that she knows without thinking about it more or less what the baby needs. She does this, in health, without losing her own identity. (Winnicott, 1988, p. 259)

Note Winnicott's insistence that the mother should provide not only adequate holding for the child but also that she should do so "without losing her own identity." Good mothering does not mean *perfect* mothering, in which the mother would presumably always be available to the infant, meeting its every need almost before it arises. A so-called perfect mother would have to forgo and forget her own identity, needs, and boundaries. The paradox here, of course, is that such total self-abnegation is not only not perfect, but it is also unhealthy.

Such *perfect* treatment of the infant is fatally flawed because it does not allow the infant to experience those moments of opposition that are necessary for it to negotiate—in monitored, bite-sized servings, of course—so that it can grow. What is more, such a hypersensitive mother becomes depleted, possibly becoming mentally and emotionally ill, and winds up with little left to give her child. Perfectionism is a one-way ticket to breakdown.

Another, even more serious, consequence of perfectionism is that the mother who becomes so psychologically enmeshed with her child—forfeiting her own limits and needs to the point of losing her own identity—will be modeling for her infant a neurotic example of what relationship means.

In the child's eyes, relationship comes to mean subservience to another to the point of having to squash his own legitimate needs in order to pander to, the self-serving excesses of others. Thus, Winnicott devised the term "good-enough mothering." By acknowledging the importance of her own legitimate, indeed crucial, needs and identity, "good-enough mothering gives opportunity for the steady development of personal processes in the baby" (Winnicott, 1988, p. 456)—processes that will allow the child to feed positively upon the mother's realistic humanity and not her neurotic perfectionism.

Of course, good-enough mothering is still loving and mindful of the infant's physical and emotional needs. However, it also recognizes the importance of the mother allowing, even encouraging, the child to become increasingly independent. With expanding autonomy, the infant, and then the older child, comes to physically and emotionally take in the existentially necessary lesson that there is a division between his inner world of Me and the outer world of Not-Me. This raises another set of dynamics that Winnicott brilliantly explores in his work.

To deal with the space between the world of Me and Not-Me, the infant, notes Winnicott, will often adopt a *transitional object*. To take a prime example: The infant's own thumb, which replaces the mother's breast when the infant wishes to nurse but mother is not available for feeding, is the first transitional object. The thumb, through a basic exercising of the infant's still-primitive imagination, comes to replace the absent breast.

In other words, the thumb is no longer just a thumb to the infant, although the child does not mistake it for a breast either. Rather, the thumb takes on the status of a transitional object. It grows into a psychologically living symbol that the child employs to satisfy at least some of its needs. Often a comfortable blanket becomes a surrogate for the mother. The child's imagination turns the blanket into a transitional object that is now not just a blanket or the mother but an imaginative fusion of both. This not only provides comfort to the child but also represents a first step in *the ability to think symbolically*. This is a watershed mark in its cognitive and psychological maturation.

As the child develops, he chooses more complex transitional objects to symbolically express and deal with the existential gap between his inner and outer realities. In a sense, therefore, all of our philosophical and artistic products, our concepts and images, are highly evolved transitional objects through which we express our fundamental existential need to interpret and interact with external reality in symbolic terms.

In transitional spaces in the classroom, a transitional object is the thing, person, or idea where the inner "I" and the outer "Other" interact to produce a "Third Pedagogical Space," as the authors call it, where human creativity always has the potential of blossoming. This can happen even in the most difficult of circumstances, as in the case of the Jewish psychiatrist Viktor Frankl (1957), whose life-altering experience of the Divine occurred within the confines of a concentration camp in World War II. This experience resulted in decades of productive work after he survived those years that were both hellish and visionary.

Finally, Winnicott suggests that *a culture may be seen as a collective transitional social object* allowing its members to share their mediated experience of reality, converse about it and within it, and thereby find ways of collectively steering it into more humane directions.

Educational Implications and Applications of Winnicott's Thought

The first application of Winnicott's work to educational theory and practice lies in the notion of good holding environments. What kind of environment does the teacher create for her students?

Does she create a space where a student feels recognized and valorized for who he really is, cognitively "held" by the teacher in such a way that he both feels free to explore new cognitive areas and trusts that she will monitor and warn him if he starts wandering off into fields that are "out-land-ish" and potentially harmful to himself and others?

Does he engage in this intellectual journey in a basic sense of both his goodness and his natural limitations—that is, with both courage and humility? Does he judiciously but joyfully anticipate the intrigue of the conceptual territory that lies just outside the boundaries of his present conceptual world?

Is there a sense of solidarity among the students bred of the surety that they are engaged in a joint venture, creating a "community of learners? (Brown, Collins, & Duguid, 1988). If so, the teacher has probably created a good pedagogical holding environment that promotes the security, boldness, and realism that the mother has engendered in her developing child.

Or does the teacher (sometimes herself the victim of oppressive corporate demands on her from the school administration as well as from depersonalizing educational policies) create a dangerous space where the student fears being labeled as incapable or even ridiculed as stupid if he does not slavishly conform to her authoritarian view of what is "right" and what is "wrong" and score high on standardized tests?

Standardized educational systems that not only do not affirm the student as a unique individual but also demand that he simply bow down to unchallenged authority in order to get good grades are all too common now, and indeed *have* been since the first real establishment of public schools in U.S. history just after the Civil War (Cremin, 1988).

If the classroom is a "bad holding environment," the student becomes a "false self," who suffers under the agony of having turned himself into something he is not in order to win a financial or social reward. For this, ultimately, is what a standardized grade is—namely, the promise of wealth, power, and prestige after schooling by filling a desirable role that conforms to a corporate, commodity-obsessed plan for the organization of society.

The great educator and educational theorist Paulo Freire (1970) has aptly called this "the banking model" of education. In the banking model of education, the teacher is like the owner of a bank who holds all its intellectual capital in his power in the form of state-approved "knowledge" in what Eisner (1985) has called "the official curriculum."

The banker will give the student some of the bank's capital in the form of a good grade, which represents a certain degree of intellectual capital now transferred to the student. To get that capital, however, the student must always agree with the banker on any and every subject, prove that he does so on standardized assessments of the student's "knowledge," and promise to use his capital only in ways that will conform to the banker's worldview. When this is the case, the curriculum is a means of personal, political, and cultural oppression and the classroom a site of servitude.

However, when the classroom is a good holding environment, the way of going about things is cooperative, not corporate. The teacher, as the master learner, and the students, as her "cognitive apprentices," learn together in a joint adventure of joyful growth (Brown, Collins, & Duguid, 1988).

This does not mean that students will always agree with each other in the conclusions they reach and the uses to which they put their individually appropriated knowledge. It does mean, however, that they will have all reached their conclusions in open and civil discourse with each other and with the teacher, for such discourse characterizes a functional democracy. Indeed, as Dewey always insisted, such discourse *is* a democracy. When this discourse happens in a classroom, then, as Dewey noted, the classroom becomes nothing less than a "laboratory of democracy" (Dewey, 1916).

For all this to happen, the teacher must have created a good holding environment, one in which students feel that they are seen as individuals whose specific needs and potential are honored and worked with. It is an educational milieu where the relevance of knowledge to a student's life is key. It is also a place where "failure" is seen simply as an opportunity to try again in a more innovative and effective approach to a question or problem.

As we have maintained various times already in this book, teaching and learning are laden with emotion. Teachers and students are not machines performing merely logical operations with emotional frigidity upon an ideologically neutral curriculum. This so-called scientific model of education is not even what truly creative scientists do, according to the great historian of science and physicist Thomas Kuhn (1970) for their work is also shot through with their emotions, commitments, specific goals, and particular worldviews.

In other words, cognition is "hot" (Pintrich, Marx & Boyle, 1993). There is scarcely a concept that is not crackling with our hopes, fears, needs, and impulses. The classroom as a good holding environment builds on this to create a stimulating community of discourse in which each student enters into living dialogue with other students and with a living curriculum in order to rise to ever new levels of integral personhood and forward-moving productivity. This kind of education for psychological integration and social cohesiveness is, we believe, the only education worthy of a democracy. The other is miseducation—education for totalitarianism.

We used the phrase "living curriculum" earlier. That may strike the reader as strange. After all, isn't a curriculum a sort of predetermined "object" or a fixed protocol to be "delivered" to students in the course of a term? It is true, of course, that what is to be read and discussed in class is usually fairly well laid out on the syllabus at the beginning of a term—although even this may change in more flexible learning environments. However, even when the curriculum is "set" in this way, it can still be either a living or a dead thing.

It is dead when it is presented to the student in such a way that it is something just to be memorized, unquestioned, reproduced as a set of one-and-only correct answers on a standardized test, and tangential at best to the student's actual life.

As the greatest of all American educational philosophers, John Dewey, said in his classic study *Democracy and Education*, such "learning" never sticks (1916). The student (quite understandably—sometimes, frankly, even healthily!) forgets the information as soon as the test is over. The student's interest in and interaction with the material is, Dewey insisted, the prime motivator of real learning, and the relationship of the student to the curriculum will vary from student to student to form a unique "subjective curriculum" for each student (Cohler, 1989).

On the other hand, the living curriculum is one in which the individual student and the class as a whole engage with the material under the teacher's expert guidance—not under the threat of a punishing grade or the demeaning seduction of a high grade. Rather, the curriculum becomes a means for the student to collaborate with other students in authentic relationship as each one internalizes knowledge in a way that builds up and enriches his sense of the world and his place in it. In Winnicottian terms, therefore, the curriculum is a living thing when it is a *transitional object* of growth, not a punitive tool of control.

"But," the teacher legitimately might ask, "where the emotional and ethical stakes in the classroom are so high, where not only my students' but also my life narrative will be so impacted by what goes on in the classroom, what if I make a mistake, even a very serious one, that will have grave consequences for all involved? How can I handle this pressure? Is it fair to tell me that I cannot be a good teacher unless I expose myself to this potential catastrophe?" Again, Winnicott comes to our aid with the notion of the good-enough mother, who, in the healthy holding environment of the classroom, becomes *the good-enough teacher.*

Inevitably, the teacher will make mistakes. She has her own limits, issues, past hurts, and future anxieties that will cause her to stumble occasionally, even fail.[2] But as long as she "holds" the classroom in relative emotional safety and fundamentally has a genuine regard for her students, she will, like the good-enough mother, present a model for them of what a fully human, fully creative individual is. In doing this, she becomes a crucial component in her students' liberation from the chains of perfectionism and conformism so that they may walk and create freely on the landscape of their ever-expanding humanity and wisdom.

The good-enough teacher, in the holding environment that she both *creates* and *is*, transforms not only the curriculum but also the entire classroom into a transitional space in which the student come to know himself, his fellow travelers, and the boundless knowledge they all pursue, in ever greater degrees of independence and innovation.

Exercises in Reflectivity Using Winnicott's Ideas

Exercise 1: As you think of your present classroom practices as a teacher or imagine what they will be in the future, how do/could you create a good holding environment? What are the major attitudes you could take, visions you could nurture both within yourself and your students, and even ways of physically designing the classroom that would turn your educational space into a good holding environment?

Exercise 2: Think of a teacher from your past or present experience as a student who was a good-enough teacher who created a good holding environment in which you grew not only intellectually but also emotionally, ethically, and politically. In your journal, write her a letter in which you mention the specific ways in which she accomplished this and thank her for this influence on you as a teacher and as a human being.

Exercise 3: Think of a teacher from your past or present who created a hostile learning environment. If you are willing to engage in this, be prepared to do a Gestalt dialogue with her in front of class in which you (1) tell her how you feel about the classroom she created and the effect it had on you and then (2) switch roles and address yourself from her point of view. If you choose to engage in this work in front of class along with a few other willing participants, you will help both yourself and others understand why some teachers are prone to bad holding of their students as well as what in oneself may resonate with these authoritarian impulses. The purpose of this exercise is not to punish oneself or others. It is, rather, to understand, forgive, and move forward with more empathic and dynamic pedagogical practices.

Exercise 4: The authors make much in this chapter of the image of the teacher as a nurturing mother. They have pointed out the benefits to both the teacher and student of internalizing this maternal image of oneself as an educator. However, do you see any shortcomings or even dangers in this approach to being a teacher? As a class, discuss what some of these might be and what, if anything, can be done to eliminate or at least control those dangers.

MARTIN BUBER

In his twentieth-century masterpiece *I and Thou* (Buber, 1965), the towering Jewish theologian Martin Buber makes it clear that the pronoun "I" was empty of meaning if it is conceived of as ever really standing alone. "I" is devoid of any sense except as it is always implicitly being coupled with one of two other pronouns in what Buber called the two primal word-units: *I-Thou* and *I-It*.

When a person says "I," is he doing so in the sense of himself as an individual in ethically perceptive and emotionally engaged relationship with another human being? Or is he doing so in the sense of himself as an individual who is simply using another human being for instrumental purposes in order to advance selfish interests in a program of control and exploitation of the other?

If the former is the case, then the "I," in a genuine honoring of the other person as a unique and divinely significant *subject,* is finding and refining himself as another unique and divinely significant *subject* in profound and passionate discourse with the other. This is the "I" in the I-Thou primal pairing. However, if the latter is the case, then the "I," in a false communion that is meant to turn the other into an *object,* demeans himself in the process, becomes less than human, and thus transforms himself into an object too. I-Thou relationship is the core of morality. I-Thou nonrelationship is the core of immorality.

But this is not all. A person who honors the divine within his dialogical partner is finding the Transcendent in the best way (indeed, the only way) possible of knowing He/She/It—namely in how one handles the sacredness of human relationships. This, felt Buber, is the essence of Judaism.

He was not alone among great Jewish thinkers in believing this. Perhaps the greatest of all rabbis, the fourth-century teacher Rabbi Akiva, summed up the wisdom of Judaism by saying that it all boiled down to loving God with all one's heart and loving one's neighbor as oneself. Buber held that this was not merely the essence of Judaism but was the essence of universal morality—to discover one's own dignity in honoring the dignity in the other.

A realist, Buber was no sunshiny optimist with a peaches-and-cream view of things. A post-Holocaust Jew and man of the world, he certainly understood that there are times when one engages in true I-Thou discourse with the other by pointing out the flaws in the other's thoughts or their lack of generosity. Sometimes, one must even expose what is bestial and cruel in another. But this was a message always to be delivered in authenticity and civility, aiming at the ultimate good for the other person, not tearing him down in strip-and-burn accusations and poisonous invectives.

Only the person whose relationship with others is of the I-Thou variety could hope to have an open and supporting relationship with the Transcendent, Buber proclaimed. Those who exploit others—sexually, emotionally, mentally, politically, or in any other way—sever the tie between themselves and the Divine.

Perhaps you, the reader, have already thought of how similar Buber's theological ideas are to the psychological ideas of Kohut and Winnicott. Like those psychological theorists, Buber gauges a person's happiness and goodness by how intellectually and emotionally abundant a person's relationships with others are. For Buber, however, the central human need for varying degrees and types of intimate relationships is not rooted in psychodynamic processes. Rather, it is the defining fact about what it means to be a human being in the first place. It is the existential nature of relationship, not its psychodynamic mechanisms, that concerned Buber.

Educational Implications and Applications
of Buber's Thought[3]

The essence of ethical teaching, said Buber, who, a great teacher, wrote a great deal on education, is fully engaged dialogue between the teacher and the student. By dialogue he meant more than simply lively conversation, although that is certainly a part of it. "Dialogue" as he used the word means a worldview that honors the basic human need and moral imperative to relate to our fellow humans in ways that are as spiritually, ethically, emotionally, and intellectually real and resonant.

Buber wrote that "the relation in education is one of pure dialogue" (1965, p. 75). He saw relationship as both the basic process and crowning goal of any learning situation. He also claimed that the cultivation of such relationships was the cornerstone of valid moral reasoning and vital ethical behavior. Hence, he made this "dialogical ethics" the foundation of his pedagogy. In fact, for Buber teaching, relationship, and spirituality are often indistinguishable from each other. "The extended lines of relation meet in the eternal *Thou*," he wrote in *I and Thou* :

> Every particular *Thou* is a glimpse through to the eternal *Thou;* by means of every particular *Thou,* the primary word addresses the eternal *Thou*. Through the mediation of the *Thou* of all beings, fulfillment, and non-fulfillment, of relations comes to them: The inborn *Thou* is realized in each relation and consummated in none. (Buber, 1965, p. 75)

Yet, because we gain access to the Divine only to the degree that we see and respond to divinity in the "other," we close the door on the Divine whenever we deny and denigrate that "other." Thus, it is that in deeply ethical educational processes the teacher enters into a relationship with the student which brings both the teacher and student into ever closer moral encounter in what the authors call "a pedagogical covenant." The subject matter under analysis in the classroom is the curricular scaffold for this ethical process—a process that illuminates the subject matter but also transcends it as the teacher and student, through dialogical encounter, approach the Transcendent.

Whatever sets itself up against relationship in education not only does moral violence but also pedagogical violence, for the teacher and student both achieve ever subtler understandings of the subject matter only as they explore it *together*. Knowledge in a vacuum is no knowledge at all—or at least, it is not fully *human* knowledge.

Educational scenarios, such as those defined in the Reagan administration's *Nation at Risk* report, and carried forward in *No Child Left Behind*, both of which considered "the basic purposes of schooling" to be primarily the reestablishment of America's "once unchallenged preeminence in commerce, industry, science and technological innovation," continue to shape U.S. educational policy and practices. They work against the spirit in education, measuring the teacher and student in the clinically anonymous terms of standardized, norm-referenced instrumentation.

This is not to assert that teaching should not also be practical. In fact, parents expect teachers to arm children with pragmatic skills and knowledge that will help them survive in the marketplace. This is an understandable and necessary requirement in a (post)industrial society. But when such purposes force themselves upon teachers and student as the centerpiece of a nationally framed agenda—becoming "the basic purposes of education" virtually to the exclusion of anything else—then education is in serious trouble.

As Cliff has argued in his previous books, this is the primary cause of many teachers' disillusionment with and abandonment of American public education. Many teachers', if not most teachers', sense of calling grows out of the primary word "I-Thou," out of their need to engage, excite, nurture, and shape the burgeoning hearts and minds of their young students. However, most corporate reform agendas grow out of the primary word "I-It" in their ceaseless and careless program of maximizing profits and dominating markets.

As Karl Marx saw, this is ultimately a cultural project of objectifying its members—members who are being increasingly conditioned not only to be *addicted* to commodities but also to *become* commodities. This is the false god of I-It triumphant. Schools become cites of commercial training and conditioning—places where teachers and students are treated, and so come to treat each other, as objects.

Lawrence Cremin the greatest of all U.S. educational historians, suggested, in his magisterial 2,000-page study of the history of American public schooling, that the educating that goes on in public schools is coming to resemble ever more closely the educating that goes on in military and commercial sites.

President Eisenhower warned about the dangers of what he called the military-industrial complex. Now, it is high time, wrote Cremin, to start worrying about the growth of a military-industrial-*educational* complex. The world-historical goal of this complex is the commodification of the "global village"—as it is slyly called in such deceptively rustic and falsely friendly terms. This project of commodification of self and others Marx called "object fetishism." In biblical terms, it is the worship of the golden calf—a problem that occupied Buber with his rabbinical mind.

The single antidote to this psychosocial illness in its many forms is the "I-Thou" relationship. In few instances is the antidote more potentially effective than in the educational relationship. Where teachers and students mutually construct ways of learning and growing together within the sacred precinct of "I-Thou," they are thereby engaged in a spiritual act of political resistance.

The teacher's mission, Buber felt, is prophetic: She reminds her students (and thus ultimately her people) that "if a man lets it have the mastery, the continuing growing world of *It* overruns him and robs him of the reality of his own *I*, till the incubus over him and the ghost within him whisper to one another the confession of their non-salvation" (Buber, 1965, p. 46).

The burden and the true "business" of education is nothing less than salvation insofar as the educative relationship brings teacher and student—through the medium of curriculum and the intensity of mutuality—into a deepening involvement with each other, and therefore with the Divine. And let us not forget that it is only such a genuine appreciation of each individual as unique that Democracy can flourish, for it is the sanctity of the individual upon which American democracy rests.

Exercises in Reflectivity Using Buber's Ideas

Exercise 1: Think of a teacher who interacted with you as a "Thou." Think also of a teacher who treated you as an "It." In your journal, contrast these two teachers in terms of interactions with them that you recall. How have these teachers differentially affected you in the years since you had them in class? As you think deeply on this issue, write about some of the consequences they have had on your larger life-narrative about what you went on to do or not to do and how you see yourself as a learner now.

Exercise 2: Some commentators on Buber have suggested that there is a third category of relationship: *I and You*. They point out that in our busy, organizationally based societies, we cannot always interact with a person as a "Thou" and must sometimes, in fact, deal with a person as an "It" for statistical or efficiency reasons. Lying between the two extremes is the I-You relationship, which, although authentic and respectful and even caring, must also be businesslike and somewhat impersonal in order to get necessary tasks done. In a class-wide discussion, consider if the I-You relationship has a place in the classroom. If so, what, if any, are instances where an I-You relationship with students is the best way for the teacher to go about doing what she needs to get done in a classroom, allowing her to avoid treating students impersonally but also not getting overwhelmed in emotion?

Exercise 3: To the degree you feel comfortable doing so, share stories in groups of four or five people about your favorite I-Thou teacher and your most harmful I-It teacher. Help each other process what effect both of these teachers may have had on your decision to become a teacher and your current ways of teaching or ways in which you presently imagine you *will* teach.

Exercise 4: For some people, the idea of a connection with the Transcendent in their teaching may seem far-fetched and irrelevant at best and an imposition on their nonreligious worldview at worst. As a general discussion involving the whole class, explore this issue with reference to First

Amendment provisions about neither encouraging nor prohibiting religion in the classroom. The authors believe that so long as a teacher is simply reflecting on the spiritual dimensions of her teaching in private and with other teachers who wish to engage in this kind of activity to become better and more fulfilled teachers, it is appropriate and does not introduce religion into the classroom. Do you agree with the authors—and why or why not?

PAUL TILLICH

In a sense, no one is an atheist, said Tillich, for at the deepest core of one's life are some foundational beliefs that ethically and philosophically guide that person's life—whether or not that person is clearly aware of them or even aware of them at all. These are the individual's "ultimate concerns," an idea introduced in the introduction chapter (Tillich, 1956).

One's ultimate concerns, says Tillich, *are* functionally equivalent to one's "god," for they are what a person considers final and finally valuable, both the source and goal of value. This has been a traditional definition of God for thousands of years, at least in the monotheistic traditions.

To become ever more aware of one's "ultimate concerns," to find ways to make them grow in insight and intensity, and to live in ever greater fidelity to them—this, said Tillich, is true spirituality.

By this measure, whether or not one professes belief in "God" is not really the question. By Tillich's reckoning, Person A who espouses a specific religious faith but has not looked at either that faith or himself very clearly and does not live according to what he professes to believe is not a spiritual person, or at least is not living a spiritual life. On other hand, Person B who calls himself an atheist is spiritual, according to Tillich, if he lives in ever-widening circles of inner clarity and service to others. Since a fair number of teachers see a spiritual side to their work, we will use Tillich's idea to help them clarify and intensify that dimension of their labor of love.

Educational Implications and Applications of Tillich

Tillich's notion of "ultimate concern" has much to tell us about what it ideally means to be a teacher, what it ideally means to be a student, and what a curriculum might optimally be.

The called teacher typically feels that her work is tied into something greater than herself, even that it serves this greater "force." Indeed, this is a key characteristic of what it means to be called to any profession—that a greater and beneficent "force" is beckoning one into the work at hand. Cliff remembers reading the memoirs of a great professor of English literature who was also a poet—and also his uncle. He wrote in an autobiography: "I chose literature (or literature chose me) just after returning from the South Pacific in World War Two."

This professor of literature and poet did not "believe" in "God." In fact, he was well known for his agonizing atheism. As an American Jew, the professor felt that the concentration camps had killed any illusion that there was a God who loved his children.

Still, as he told Cliff during a walk one very chilly night in Stockton, California, at the University of the Pacific in 1974 where his uncle was a professor and Cliff was a student, he felt that in some way he could not understand but still believed in, he had been destined to be a literature teacher and poet. It was the action of "something" *greater* than himself.

Now, it doesn't matter much if one names the source of that calling "God," something else, or nothing at all, for it is clear in any case that the origin of my uncle, the professor-poet's sense of calling was in a region that transcended himself while at the same time being central within himself. His calling was so interwoven with his sense of "ultimacy" in life that the two could be separated. Teaching was integral to his life narrative.

"But," you might say, "it's different with professors. They have so much free time and other benefits that K–12 teachers don't have." This is true. However, as the two authors of this book can attest, university teaching has its own unique trials, politics, and demands that can pose a substantial threat to the integrity of the professor's sense of calling as a teacher. In any case, in almost every educational site, there are enough challenges to one's integrity as a teacher that they threaten to sever the living connection between one's teaching and one's life as a whole.

When that happens, the teacher becomes alienated from her work, and either cynicism or leaving the field inevitably follows. As a teacher educator in not only the United States but also in Asia and Central America over the past thirty-five years, Cliff has found that most teachers choose their work because it is ethically pivotal to their lives, and that they will leave their work if they no longer feel that this is the case. Indeed, it is largely to help deal with the problem of teacher alienation that we have written this book. Tillich is extraordinarily helpful here. He reminds us all that there is nothing as important as finding and continually deepening one's sense of ultimacy and then (we would add) manifesting it in one's teaching.

There is no easy or readymade formula for how to accomplish this in terms of one's profession. Clearly, it is finally an intensely personal matter to determine how one's life as a teacher is organically tied into one's life as a whole. It is also a deeply individual issue to discover what in one's present teaching situation nurtures one's sense of ultimacy, what threatens it, and what one should do to promote the former and resist the latter. However, let us suggest a few things to try alone and in class that may aid you in this crucial endeavor.

Exercises in Reflectivity Using Tillich's Idea

Exercise 1: In your journal, list some of your most important values. For example, being a loyal friend may be particularly significant to you. You might also especially value being a supportive mate to your life partner if you have one. If you have children, you'll almost certainly rank your nurturance and guidance of them at the top of the list. What it means to be a member of a pluralistic democracy might also occupy you deeply. After writing down your top four to five values, try to see what they might have in common, what seems to lie at the point where they all intersect as in a Venn diagram. Doing this might help you further clarify your core values—or *ultimate concerns*.

Exercise 2: In a follow-up to the preceding exercise, be prepared to discuss your ultimate concerns with a dialogical partner. Listen to each other as deeply, reflectively, and nonjudgmentally as you can, aiming at a true I-Thou conversation. Help each other process how your present or future teaching situation might relate positively and/or negatively to your essential values. Help each other imagine ways that might help you protect and deepen your ultimate concerns as teachers in the classroom.

Exercise 3: In a classroom where the teacher and students are simply "Its" (with the teacher delivering a standardized curriculum and the student memorizing the right answers for the test), the curriculum is by definition also an "It" because it is fixed and lifeless. On the other hand, in an I-Thou classroom, the curriculum becomes dynamic, responsive, and an occasion for ever new explorations into subject matter and self. Taking a standard topic from the area in which you teach or will teach, discuss in groups some of the differences in how you would represent that topic on the syllabus and how you would present it in class if you were taking an I-Thou approach.

ABRAHAM MASLOW

Maslow's early model of the psyche, taught in most Psych 101 classes near the end of the term, is well known. It posited a pyramid of needs, starting at the base with physiological needs and then ascending to safety needs, followed by belongingness needs, esteem needs, cognitive needs, aesthetic needs, and culminating in self-actualization needs. These are quite parallel to the psychological dynamics featured in Kohut's and Winnicott's self-psychological systems, especially in the self-actualization needs at the peak of the pyramid.

Indeed, Maslow was instrumental in launching discussions in the late 1960s and early 1970s about education as the therapeutic pursuit of the student's *self*-identity. He declared during the height of his early, self-actualization period, in words that capture both the spirit of self-based psychologies and the relationship of teaching and therapy, that

> if we want to be helpers, counselors, teachers, guides, or psychotherapists, what we must do is to accept the person and help him learn what kind of person he is already. What is his style, what are his aptitudes, what is the person good for, not good for, what can we build upon, what are his good raw materials, his potentialities?. . . Above all, we would care for the child, that is, enjoy him and his growth and his self-actualization. (1968, p. 47)

However, what is less generally known is that around 1968 Maslow began to feel that this ego-based model, despite its existential richness, was wanting.

Above self-actualization needs, Maslow started to perceive the inherent human need *to go beyond ego*, to forge a link with "the naturalistically transcendent, spiritual, and axiological" (Maslow, 1968, pp. iii–iv). He called this "religion with a little 'r.'" It required no adherence to any religious dogma. It was universal, he claimed—an inherent and defining characteristic of the human being as such.

Maslow came to feel that without spiritually invigorating communication with this realm, the psyche would ultimately grow restless, hungry, and would become shrunken, dry, and pathological. This was as true in therapy as in education, he asserted. This idea insists upon the significance of not only the personal realm of experience but also the *trans*personal realm.

Maslow asserted that a complete picture of the human psyche must not only include issues from one's *personal* history but also aim at accessing *transpersonal* realities that inform both cosmos and psyche—realities that are perennial, universal, and that incarnate in the *conjoined* psyche and spirit. This would take place in the *psychospiritual* domain. Maslow publicly speculated in his seminal *Towards a Psychology of Being* that such a psychology would be "centred in the cosmos" and, without neglecting the personal realm, would go "beyond humanness, identity, self-actualization, and the like."

In sum, the task of engaging in psychospiritual theorizing and creating psychospiritual therapies in this new key was becoming clear to Maslow, because "without the transpersonal, we get sick, violent, and nihilistic, or else hopeless and apathetic" (1968, p. iiif).

This perspective is invaluable to us in identifying and cultivating the more spiritual aspects of the teacher's sense of calling.

Educational Implications and Applications of Maslow's Ideas

There are probably few subjects that are so inadequately explored in studying the lives of teachers as their spiritual beliefs and practices, whether those teachers are in preparation in colleges of education or already leading their own classrooms in the field. In light of Maslow's later thought, we see how unfortunate this lack of attention to spirituality is in fully grasping many teachers' sense of calling since many of us are motivated by what can only be called spiritual reasons to become teachers. Thus, we must find ways to boldly recognize, honor, and cultivate that fact in order to foster profound forms of reflectivity in ourselves as educators.

We want to make it clear, however, that we do not consider all religious practices as necessarily spiritual. Much (indeed, too much) of the practice of institutional religion is a matter of cultural conformity or social expediency. We therefore want to use the phrase "spirituality" to denote not only formal "religion" but also and equally those highly personal forms of spirituality that are an existentially authentic pursuit of a transpersonal reality—a pursuit, moreover, that hopes to contact the Timeless, resulting in personal clarity and empathic service to others.

We will adopt Cornett's (1998) six intrinsic aspects of spirituality as guidelines in engaging in reflecting spiritually upon ourselves as teachers. These involve considering: (1) the meaning of life, (2) values, (3) mortality, (4) the organization and guidance of the universe, (5) suffering, and (6) transcendence. Let us do so in the following section by engaging in a single, simple but powerful Zen meditative exercise that Cliff learned from his meditation teacher, Genpo Merzel Roshi, at the Kanzeon Zen Center almost twenty years ago. It has been adapted here to promote spiritual reflectivity as a teacher.

An Exercise in Spiritual Reflectivity (with Special Reference to Yourself as a Teacher)

Imagine that you are very old. Death is not far away. You are peacefully lying in bed awaiting its imminent arrival.

What would say to yourself now, at your actual present age, about the meaning of your life and all that you had been through in it? What is the core of it all? How should you live the rest of your life from this point on, having heard the incalculably precious words from your old wise self, who is about to pass on from this realm of existence?

Now, even more specifically, ask that old, profoundly wise "you" what your life as a teacher means from that sage perspective. How does your calling as a teacher look from that point of view? Should you go on being a teacher? If not, why not? If so, why? And again if so, what will you now—in light of this great wisdom about yourself as a teacher and how it fits into your larger life—*keep on* being and doing, *stop* being and doing, and *start* being and doing as a teacher? *Why* will you do this? *How* will you do this? *What* will this look like in your daily classroom practice?

CONCLUSION: THE PSYCHOSPIRITUALLY EVOLVING TEACHER

Hopefully, we have provided you with theories, suggestions, clues, and exercises in this chapter—drawn from their own research and lives as committed educators in their combined seventy years in the classroom—that will aid you in your own psychological and spiritual journey to ever more integrated states and ever more elevated realms from which to carry on your important work. Have no doubt that your labor impacts your students, present and future, at all levels of their being, from the physical to the spiritual, from the political and cultural to the broadly ethical. We honor and support you in your noble work.

In the next chapter, we, called teachers like you, wish to continue helping you grow in your vocation, the noblest of all professions, by introducing you to Carl Jung—scholar, psychologist, and physician.

NOTES

1 Cliff has discussed this syndrome in his own practice as a teacher and how he dealt with it in his article "Personal and Archetypal Transference and Counter-Transference in the Classroom" if you would like to take a look at it as an example of this kind of exercise in pedagogical reflectivity (Mayes, 2002).

2 Cliff deals with these questions at length in his article "The Teacher as Shaman" (Mayes, 2005).

3 This section is taken from Cliff's book *Teaching Mysteries: Foundations of a Spiritual Pedagogy* (2004) and is reproduced here with the kind permission of University Press of America: Lanham, Maryland.

Chapter Two

Jung: The Essentials

PART ONE

Jung never totally accepted Freud's insistence on the strictly sexual origin of both healthy and pathological psychodynamics, even during the height of their friendship (Shamdasani, 2003). And when, toward the end of a relatively brief but momentous association between the two men from about 1905 to 1912, Freud told Jung that the sexual hypothesis must become, as he put it, a "dogma," Jung knew that he would soon have to break with his august colleague. This was no easy move for Jung either professionally or emotionally, for Freud had named the brilliant thirty-year-old Swiss psychiatrist his "crown prince"—heir to the psychoanalytic dynasty that Freud was forging and that Jung would head after Freud someday departed.

But although Jung had been of a very mystical bent all his life, he strove as a physician to be empirical and scientific as well and always insisted that a theory should never be an article of faith. What if there were evidence pointing to other factors at play in the psyche—factors that did not deny the importance of sexuality but that put it in a more realistic place rather than insisting on it as the sole occupant of the psyche's center? Moreover, Jung asserted that reducing all human experience to coitus was both ethically and intellectually problematic.

Little by little, what the spiritually gifted Jung intuited in his mystical experiences and dreams as a boy, and what the university student Jung who argued against materialism in his debate-club speeches was beginning to conceptualize, was now coming together into a clear vision to Jung the psychiatrist. In both his scholarly studies and clinical practice he saw that the drives for sex and power (although undoubtedly important—Jung never denied that) were finally secondary. They were, as he put it, "fragments" that grew out of a layer of psyche that was, paradoxically, both deeper and higher than those that had to do with sex and power. Jung called this deeper/higher level of psyche the "primordial" layer.

By "primordial" Jung meant more than simply that this core of psyche was ancient, even inscribed in our evolutionary history—although it *was* that. He used that word to also point us toward something that was simultaneously so primary and so transcendent in the structure and dynamics of the psyche that it seemed to be spiritual almost by definition (Jung, 1967b, p. 117). But what was this as-yet undiscovered source that was the goldmine of psychic energy? What was the terrain leading to it? How would one go about exploring such a rare place? Was there a way of mapping it?

From the Personal Subconscious to the Collective Unconscious

As a young psychiatrist at the famous Burghölzli Clinic in Zurich Jung began to find clinical evidence of this territory. The rest of his life would be devoted to traveling through it in and with his patients, and in and for himself—and writing about it in essays and books that would come to make up the eighteen volumes of his writings in his *Collected Works*. The first-time reader of Jung should approach the *Collected Works* with an accessible interpretation of Jung by his side since Jung can be difficult to read (Mayes, 2016).

Jung found that this dimension of psyche showed itself most clearly in psychotic patients. He reasoned that this was because in psychosis virtually every ego-structure is shattered, leaving the person with an unfiltered vision—sometimes terrifying, sometimes exhilarating—of this overwhelming territory. Jung gives an example of one of his earliest clinical experiences of this in a fascinating story about one of his patients, a young man in his thirties whom he was treating at the Burghölzli Clinic. The man believed himself to be Christ.

> One day I came across [the young patient], blinking through the window up at the sun, and moving his head from side to side in a curious manner. He took me by the arm and said he wanted to show me something. He said that I must look at the sun with eyes half shut, and then I could see the sun's phallus. If I moved my head from side to side the sun-phallus would move too, and that was the origin of the wind. I made this observation about 1906. In the course of the year 1910, when I was engrossed in mythological studies, a book of Dietrich's came into my hands. It was part of the so-called Paris magic papyrus and was thought to be a liturgy of the Mithraic cult. It consisted of a series of instructions, invocations and visions. One of these visions is described in the following words: "And likewise the so-called tube, the origin of the ministering wind. For you will see hanging down from the disc of the sun something that looks like a tube. And

towards the regions westward it is as though there were an infinite east wind. But if the other wind should prevail towards the regions of the east, you will in like manner see the vision veering in that direction." (Jung, 1967b, pp. 150–151)

Jung noted at the time that "the parallelism of the two visions cannot be disputed." How could this "parallelism" between a schizophrenic's hallucination and an ancient creation myth be accounted for? Had this relatively uneducated young Swiss villager run across this myth before, forgotten it, and now reproduced it from his personal subconscious? Perhaps. But that seemed unlikely, and it seemed less and less likely as Jung, who was adept at various ancient languages and a student of ancient mythologies, now started to see these correspondences between individual psychic contents and mythic patterns cropping up all over the place in both his studies and his practice.

This led Jung to the assertion—one that the psychological establishment with its fixation on what is measurable refuses to seriously consider—that individuals of all sorts, and cultures of all times and all places, draw from a certainly ancient and potentially transcendent source that generates the images, themes, and stories that give voice, picture, and story to their existence. This source is the transpersonal dimension of psyche—one that does not deny the existence of the personal dimension of the psyche but gives it meaning and direction. Jung called it *the collective unconscious:*

> This discovery means another step forward in our understanding: the recognition, that is, of two layers in the unconscious. We have to distinguish between a personal unconscious and an *impersonal* or *transpersonal unconscious.* We speak of the latter also as the *collective unconscious,* because it is detached from anything personal and is common to all men, since its contents can be found everywhere, which is naturally not the case with the personal contents. The personal unconscious contains lost memories, painful ideas that are repressed . . . , subliminal perceptions that were not strong enough to reach consciousness, and finally, contents that are not yet ripe for consciousness. . . . The primordial images [of the collective unconscious], however, are the most ancient and the most universal "thought-forms" of humanity. They are as much feelings as thoughts; indeed, they lead their own independent life. (Jung, 1967b, p. 66)

In broad terms, then, Jung's model of psyche is comprised of three interacting elements: personal *consciousness,* the personal *subconscious,* and the *collective unconscious* (*CW* 8, par. 321).

Freud must be honored for his momentous work with the personal subconscious. But it was Jung who had the courage and capacity to take us to that boundary line where the individual psyche under the direction of the *ego* makes contact with the *collective, timeless* psyche. This universal and inherently spiritual force resides in the individual's deepest core—the *Self*, which is a sort of transcendent parallel of the ego.

To create a link between one's ego and one's Self—that is, between one's ordinary consciousness and one's deepest spiritual intuitions and identity—is the goal of Jungian psychotherapy. The person who can forge this inner linkage between ego and Self is effective in the world because he is dynamically balanced within himself. He has established what the great Jungian theorist Erich Neumann called an "ego-Self axis."

The Archetypes and the Collective Unconscious

Men and women have always been born with essential tendencies to hope, fear, imagine, hate, and love the same things. The idea of the collective unconscious bears powerful witness to the essential brotherhood and sisterhood of all people at all times. But what are these "most ancient and . . . most universal 'thought-forms' of humanity"—these "contents of the collective unconscious"? Jung called them *archetypes*.

The idea of an archetype is not the easiest thing to grasp—something even Jung's most fervent admirers are the first to admit (Frey-Rohn, 1974). But then again, an archetype is less a concept than a felt-knowledge of certain universal longings and aversions, hopes and fears, despairs and exaltations that move within us all—and that we move within. Being both ancient and, in a sense, timeless, the emergence of an archetype frequently engenders in us a sense of spiritual presence—the *numinous,* as Jung called it, drawing on the Greek word for spirit, *numen*. It brings us into proximity of what Rudolf Otto calls a *mysterium tremendum et fascinans*—a tremendous and fascinating mystery. It is because the archetype exists at the deepest levels of our ethical and spiritual being that Jungian psychology has been welcomed much more enthusiastically in the arts and humanities than the social sciences.

To help clarify what an archetype is, let us look at two of the most common archetypes throughout history: the archetype of *the savior* and the archetype of *the questing hero*. Because an archetype is a human universal, one would expect to find such important archetypes occurring often throughout history. And this is precisely the case with these two archetypes, as Sir James Frazer (1935) demonstrated in his classic mythological study *The Golden Bough* and Joseph Campbell (1949) in his equally seminal work *The Hero with a Thousand Faces*.

In ancient Egypt, for instance, the archetype of the savior was embodied in the form of the god Osiris, in Greece by Dionysus, and in Roman-occupied Palestine around 30 C.E. by an iterant preacher named Jesus. In all of these cases, the archetypal energy is strikingly similar. What is variable, said Jung, are the *archetypal figures*, *images*, and *events* that were used to flesh out the archetype, for this varied according to historical and cultural factors.

Hence, in this case, Osiris, Dionysus, and Jesus are historically and culturally variable *archetypal images/symbols* of the archetype of the savior. Jung speculated that part of being human is to have this attraction to savior figures because we are all born with the archetype of the savior somehow inscribed in us. That disposition constitutes an *archetype,* which will be found in almost all epochs and cultures, albeit in different *archetypal images/symbols* according to the time and place in which the individual and his culture exist.

The second example comes from a very common set of archetypes (set off in italics) consisting of the *wise old man* who, possessing *secret knowledge, magical potions, and powerful amulets,* comes to the aid of a young man at a particularly difficult passage in the youth's perilous journey through a *forest, desert, jungle, or some other danger-ridden natural landscape* as he follows *a path of many trials* in order to develop into a *hero who then returns to his culture in order to renew it.* The relationship between and adventures of Obi Wan Kenobi and Luke Skywalker fit this archetypal pattern perfectly.

Additionally, the dramas, sitcoms, and even advertisements on any given night's television programming offer numerous examples of virtually all the archetypes being embodied in everything from soap operas to sales pitches. A new branch of advertising is called "archetypal engineering." Its purpose is to dress up archetypal characters, themes, and stories in modern terms and settings in order to channel their primal power to entice consumers to buy.

Although it is unwise to be simplistic about who or what meets the standard of being an archetype, it is still possible to identify some nodal characters, themes, images, and motifs.

Some of the most important archetypes embodied as persons or animals include king, queen, trickster, lover, bride and groom, wise one/teacher, disciple, divine child, eternal child, shadow, magical helpful animal, an animal or ethnic minority sidekick, dragon/leviathan, nurturing mother, virgin, witch, harlot/temptress, Amazon, psychic medium, law-giving father, priest/priestess, evil king, rogue, warrior, senex (the grumpy old man, not a wise one), devil, and savior.

Archetypal events include birth, baptism, initiation, education, vocation, courtship, matrimony, warfare, friendship, ritual sacrifice, descent to the underworld, death, resurrection, and final judgment.

Some of the most prominent archetypal landscapes and structures are the wilderness, city, home, place of instruction, temple, battlefield, heaven, and hell.

Certain geometrical shapes are also archetypally salient: circles, squares (especially crosses), and triangles (especially in three-person godheads).

Certain numbers also seem to have particularly profound psychospiritual significance and are therefore archetypal. Jung felt that numbers are only secondarily a means of counting; their primal function is psychospiritual in that they are "an archetype of order which has become conscious" (Jung, in von Franz, 1991, p. 268f; also see Jung, 1968b, 1968c, 1968d, 1970b, Jung, 1969a, p. 456). Certainly, numbers come rich with symbolic significance when they occur in dreams. One signifies unity; two, duality; three, the reconciliation of tension in a new (i.e., third) perspective that unites but transcends the opposing polarities, like the apex of a triangle; four, the creation of a new foundation upon which the new perspective can become established; and five as the essence of the whole process—the *quint-essence*.

To sum up, the collective unconscious is the source out of which all our subconscious dynamics come—and from which, as Cliff has argued elsewhere, even our conscious thought processes stem (Mayes, 2016). Where this source "resides" is a matter of speculation. Is it an "inner" process? Does it come from an ontologically real "outer" source? Are both of these things true? Or is the term "collective unconscious" itself merely a kind of poetic image, a term of convenience that we use simply to be able to account for the striking similarities in characters/events/plots/themes that we observe when we compare widely disparate cultures' foundational narratives, and then when we compare *those* with the dreams and issues of individual, especially regarding deeply rooted psychodynamic issues that those individuals are having?

The same questions present themselves when we try to grasp what archetypes—which are, in a sense, the psychospiritual "building blocks" of the collective unconscious—are. Again, we must use what may finally be just a convenient metaphor in picturing an archetype as a packet or pattern of supercharged energy in constant and complex interactions with other such packets or patterns of energy within the "field" of the collective unconscious.

Through the archetypes, we—both as individuals and as members of a culture—make sense out of and give form to our inner and outer worlds regarding practices and themes that have proven constant throughout history and across cultures, although how we do so varies along historical, cultural, and personal lines.

The specific characters, images, and stories that result from this mysterious, compelling process and embody it in countless ways are *archetypal symbols* that seem to cluster into groups around certain basic *archetypes*.

Jung's Contributions to Ego-psychology

It is beyond question that Jung was the first modern Western psychologist to deal extensively and somewhat systematically with realms of psyche that transcend the ego—that is, that are *trans-egoic, transpersonal*. Moving into such realms of psyche means that it is no longer enough merely to talk only about *psychodynamic processes* but also *psychospiritual dynamics*.

Yet it is also true, though often forgotten, that Jung never lost sight of the *personal* nature of the psyche—its ordinary focus on sex, status, and power—and his contributions to ego-psychology in the twentieth century are substantial. Let us look at some of the major ideas and terms in ego-psychology that come from Jung. (In the next chapter, we will move into Jung's more distinctly archetypal contributions.) The first one of Jung's ideas that has gained popularity in ego-psychology is the now-popular notion of the *persona*.

Persona

Jung defined a *persona* as one of the wide array of masks that we don for others to see of us to assure them (and perhaps mostly to assure ourselves!) that we are "alright" and that we know and play by the given rules of social interaction in a particular situation. Since we all fill so many roles in our lives, it is simply a fact of social life that an individual has not just one *persona* but many of them. Creating and wearing *personas* is what the sociologist Ervin Goffman called "face work" (Goffman, 1997).

Having *personas* is not in itself a bad thing, according to Jung. It is, in fact, necessary because we must all negotiate the day-to-day world and cooperate with others in many different ways and settings. As the great nineteenth-century American psychologist William James said, the *persona* is the "me"—what I want others to perceive when they look at me. But my understanding of the full range of myself as a conscious being is my "I," or ego—who I believe I *really* am. I am the one who is *aware of* my personas.

We need our personas. Harmonious and productive social interactions would soon come to a grinding halt and society go up in flames if everyone went around saying exactly what he thought of everyone in every encounter throughout the day.

However, if an individual spends too much time and energy fixating on how he appears to others, he becomes *persona possessed*. He is then a fake—so obsessed with his masks, which typically have to do with his social roles and material possessions—that he has become what Winnicott calls a "false self" (1992). This is a common cause of depression and anxiety because at some level the person is tormented or deflated by the knowledge that he is betraying what he *really* is or could become.

The Shadow and the "Inferior Function"

Jung noted that his idea of the shadow was roughly equivalent to Freud's idea of the personal subconscious in some essential ways, but that it also differed from it in other important ways. "By *shadow* I mean the negative side of the personality—the sum of all those unpleasant qualities we like to hide, together with the insufficiently developed functions, and the contents of the personal unconscious" (Jung, 1967b, p. 66, n. 5).

Understandably but mistakenly, many people take Jung's idea of the shadow to mean that it is simply the dark, boarded-up junk-cellar of all that is evil in us which we do not want to see (although we are judgmentally quick to see it in others) or memories that are just too painful to keep in conscious awareness and go on functioning, as with the horror of sexual abuse or the aftermath of unspeakable events on a battlefield. These kinds of things are handled quite well by both (post-)Freudian and (post-)Jungian theory and therapy.

What makes the Jungian idea of the shadow so distinctive is that it also contains "qualities we like to hide." Those qualities and abilities may be good and creative, or at least potentially so. However, we have hidden them from others and eventually from ourselves because we have concluded that *not* to do so might put us at risk.

This often happens during childhood when the child fears, often enough with good cause, that if only a certain propensity or ability of his were known, it would offend others, typically a primary caregiver or peers. He feels that this would leave him isolated and exposed. *Shadow-work* in Jungian therapy often entails honoring the inner child's fears but assuring him that it is safe to "come out" now that his adult self is in charge and knows how to help those long-repressed elements of his authentic self emerge, develop, and even prevail in relative safety under the adult ego's accumulated wisdom and protective guidance.

Also note that Jung mentions "insufficiently developed functions" that reside in the shadow. These can be things that we feel we are not adept at.

For example, some people are not good with mechanical objects. As the very opposite of the kinds of things that such people do well—what Jung called their *superior function*—these insufficiently developed things are part of what Jung called their *inferior function*. Filling a tank of gas at the station, changing a tire, and putting in a new lightbulb or battery pretty much exhaust their range of mechanical skills—or so they have trained themselves to think. They shy away from them. But this causes them to miss out on exploring some abilities—from minor to great—they might actually be able to discover and develop within themselves.

This growth could well occur only if one would let these undeveloped abilities surface and not see it as a catastrophe whenever one *does* try to do something one does not feel good at and is unsuccessful—a syndrome known as "learned helplessness." By acknowledging but not being paralyzed by challenges in one's inferior function, whatever it may happen to be, one can often find interesting opportunities for growth in a new domain, however small or substantial that growth may prove to be.

In the reverse of the present example, some people who can fix anything and might now even make their living doing so might feel they are not able to do well academically. But if they gave it a shot and not let themselves descend into the unfruitful comfort of learned helplessness, they might marvel at what they are capable of.

In the Jungian view, it is of the utmost importance that we face and integrate our shadow and inferior function into our conscious awareness and personality. For if acknowledged and helped along, the shadow and inferior function are indispensable in aiding one in the ongoing journey to become more *whole*—more physically, emotionally, intellectually, and socially *integrated*. In this manner, one becomes more powerful because the elements that make one up are not only not at war with each other but are synergistically linked in the service of one's psychospiritual growth. Indeed, it is an important tenet of holistic psychology and education that undeveloped parts of one's personality do not lie dormant but, in protest against being neglected, turn "cancerous" and begin to invade and undermine the stronger parts of the personality.

In Jungian psychology, it is something of a psychological law that if one does not attend to one's inferior function, it will ultimately revolt because of being neglected and find ways to undermine an individual, working havoc in his life. Thus, a brilliant theoretical physicist who has devoted himself to constructing complex mathematical models of alternate universes might be undermined in his work every day because he is so accident-prone with physical things that he is always either having some sort of accident or cleaning up after one.

Jung—who was a superb stonemason, a competent chef, a reserve officer in the Swiss Army, a graphic artist, an intrepid hiker through deserts and jungles, an amateur sailor, and an avid motorist—always insisted that the holistic cultivation of oneself is an overarching purpose of life. He called this integration of various aspects of oneself into a wise and potent unity *individuation*—one of the most important concepts in Jungian psychology. What is more, Jung was always quick to insist that by "complete" and "individuated" he did not mean that the individual should become, or should even want to be, "perfect." Being whole and being perfect are two very different things.

In the exhausting push to be perfect—perfectly strong, perfectly beautiful, perfectly virtuous, perfectly orthodox, having the perfect house, perfect job, and perfect children, and always score the perfect 100 percent on the test, of course—we make inhuman demands upon ourselves and those around us. Losing our sense of humor as well as our sense of humanity, we become joyless and judgmental and wind up doing ourselves and those around us great harm. These are points that you may recall from the previous chapter in our discussion of Winnicott's "good enough mother."

Projection

Returning to the idea of the shadow, the most important reason that a person must bring his own shadow to the surface and work with it has to do with another Jungian concept that has become well known—*projection.*

Projection means that we ascribe to others undesirable things in ourselves that we do not wish to see in ourselves but prefer to avoid by pointing fingers instead. Sometimes we might be seeing such things as they actually exist in others. More often, it is probably an illusion. But that is not the point. The point is that in both cases we are avoiding taking a good hard look at what is wrong in us as individuals. "He who is without sin among you," said Jesus, "let him cast a stone" (*John* 8: 7).

To do this is to play a vicious game of psychological hide-and-seek with oneself by refusing to cast the light of honest introspection on one's own shabby parts. Such frank self-examination makes us more realistic about ourselves and more compassionate toward others. This will in turn engender a greater ability to forgive and help the other person, not sanctimoniously condemn him.

It is therefore psychologically and ethically imperative that we encounter and learn to productively deal with our shadow. This means a great deal more than just an offhanded admission that one has a dark side. "The grow-ing awareness of the inferior part of the personality," Jung wrote, "should not be twisted into an intellectual activity, for it has far more the meaning of a suffering and a passion that implicate the whole man" (Jung, 1969a, p. 208). It requires the moral courage to seek "ruthless self-knowledge" (Jung 1969c, p. 166). Indeed, "the shadow is a moral problem" because it "challenges the whole ego-personality"—especially those personalities that are either overly sweet because they refuse to look at their own darkness or overly critical because they insist on casting that darkness upon another (Jung, 1969c, p. 14).

Doing one's own shadow work is "the essential condition for any kind of self-knowledge, and it therefore, as a rule, meets with considerable resis-tance" in therapy, requiring "much painstaking work extending over a long period" (Jung, 1969c, p. 8). The work is worth the pain, however, for this "increasing psychological insight hinders the projection of the shadow," resulting in enhanced psychological and moral realism (Jung, 1970c, p. 168). In therapy, the shadow is often one of the earliest figures to emerge in the analysand's dreams, for the repressed parts of the psyche begin to "sense" that they have a safe therapeutic setting in which to come forth.

In dreams, the shadow is usually the same gender as the dreamer and often has something dark associated with it. The fact that the shadow has been "despised" by consciousness can also be symbolized in the dream by the shadow being an alien, a citizen of an opposing country, a member of a minority group, a criminal, a homeless person; or by being somehow unethical, sick, or menacing (Adams, 1996). In studying racism, sexism, and ageism, researchers from the social sciences have neglected to look at the fact that these things often involve the projection of one's own unconscious dynamics upon a marginalized individual or group.

On the other hand, research into homophobia *has* looked at prejudice as the fearful projection of an individual's homoerotic feelings onto the LGBT community—a line of research that has proven quite successful and could fruitfully be used in studying other forms of prejudice.

Just as the *persona* is the first psychic formation that greets the individual as he begins to examine how he operates in the outer social world, so the *shadow* is the first thing that he sees as he looks inwardly. In this sense, the shadow and the *persona* are the opposite poles that define the boundaries within which the ego "oscillates" in its daily operations and transformations. That is why ego psychologies in general often go no farther outward that the *persona* and no farther inward than the shadow in their theories or practices.

Projection functions mainly in the form of what Freud called *the transference* and Jung's subsequent expansion of that idea in the idea of *counter-transference*. These ideas being so crucial in depth psychology in general and Jungian psychology in particular, we now turn to an examination of them.

TRANSFERENCE AND COUNTER-TRANSFERENCE: PERSONAL AND ARCHETYPAL

Personal Transference

Decades after his first meeting with Freud in March 1907, Jung recalled the event:

> After a conversation lasting many hours there came a pause. Suddenly he asked me out of the blue, "And what do you think about the transference?" I replied with the deepest conviction that it was the alpha and omega of the analytical method, whereupon he said, "Then you have grasped the main thing." (Jung, 1992, p. 8)

What is this "main thing" that Freud and Jung agreed was the centerpiece of depth psychology? It is called "the transference." In the classical Freudian view the transference is the projection of "feelings, drives, attitudes, fantasies, and defenses toward a person in the present which are inappropriate to that person and are a repetition, a displacement of reactions originating in regard to significant persons of early childhood" (Greenson, 1990, p. 151).

In other words, the transference is, as Freud put it in a now-famous phrase, "a new edition" of an old problem because the patient projects issues (typically regarding parents and other primary caregivers) from his early childhood onto the psychotherapist (Freud, 1970, p. 462). In therapy the primary goal is for the therapist to help the analysand see what is going on and, bringing this unhealthy dynamic to conscious awareness, thus help liberate the analysand from this compulsion—so destructive to both self and other.

The therapist must be able to "contain" the transference neurosis of the patient, therefore, in such a way that the patient can play the old issues out again but this time resolve them satisfactorily in the consulting room with a safe person who is aware of this dynamic but is able to direct the patient toward transcending it, not remaining compulsively stuck in it.

As just mentioned, in classical psychoanalysis the significant persons of early childhood are typically the mother and father, and the "person in the present," the analyst. Hence, a male analysand's relationship to the male or female analyst will reflect the nature of the analysand's relationship to his own mother and father in the specific Oedipal dynamics that psychically (mis)shaped him. The same dynamics are at play for the female analysand, of course, except that they revolve around the female's presumed "Electra" desire for psychophysical union with her father instead of the male's Oedipal desire for psychophysical merger with the mother.

Although the theories of the Oedipus and (especially) Electra complexes have been challenged by some, most views of the transference still revolve around the classical Freudian postulation of the analysand's symbolic displacement of primary problems regarding some significant figure in his early life onto someone in the present.

Freud spoke of the transference as being either *positive* or *negative*, for the analysand will project either affectionate or hostile emotions onto the analyst depending upon the analysand's original feelings toward the figure in her past whom the analyst symbolizes. Freud thus distinguished "a 'positive' transference from a 'negative' one, the transference of affectionate feelings from that of hostile ones" (Freud, 1990, p. 32). For Freud, of course, the transference was always erotic at its core. Although the sexual component of the transference was "undeniable," according to Jung, "it is not always the only one and not always the essential one" (1992, p. 9).

One of Jung's greatest interpreters, Michael Fordham, sums Jung's view of the matter up perfectly when he says the transference involves other "moral, social and ethical components [of the analysand's psychic functioning] which become the analyst's allies once they have been 'purged' of their 'regressive components, their infantile sexualism'" (1996, p. 115). In other words, the analysand may project "psychic contents" onto the analyst, which are not necessarily (or at least not *primarily*) sexual. Indeed, the projection by the analysand onto the analyst may not be personal at all (or only personal in part). It may be *transpersonal and archetypal*. The analysand may, in other words, be projecting archetypal energy and imagery onto the analyst.

Transpersonal Transference

Just as it is probably inevitable that an analysand will project *personal* sub-conscious contents onto the analyst, she will probably project *transpersonal* unconscious contents onto the therapist, too. Some Jungians even maintain that "archetypal transference" is at the heart of any therapeutic situation (Knox, 1998). If this is true, then at the center of every personal "complex" is a transpersonal, archetypal core, whose power radiates from the depths of the collective unconscious and permeates the individual's unique identity and issues. It is an instance *par excellence* of the interaction of the universal and particular—the *collective unconscious*, on one hand, with the individual's *personal subconscious* and *ego consciousness*, on the other hand.

For example, if a male analysand is projecting mother-issues onto a female therapist, it may turn out that it is not only his personal, Oedipal issues that he is projecting. At the transpersonal level of the collective unconscious, he may simultaneously be under the sway of the seductive appeal exerted by the archetypal Great Mother back into the cosmic womb, what Freud called *Thanatos*—the desire to dwell in oblivion (Neumann, 1954).

Bringing this to conscious awareness is an example of encouraging ego and archetype to communicate with each other in that ego-Self axis, which, as we have already discussed, is another earmark of individuation (Edinger, 1973). This can go far in revitalizing the patient's life and creating in him a deepened sense of significance and an enlarged capability for creative action in the world since he is now drawing more directly upon archetypal energy—another aspect of individuation.

Personal and Transpersonal Counter-Transference

Just as the analysand projects psychic issues onto the analyst, so the ana-lyst may (and, again, perhaps inevitably does) project his psychic issues back onto the analysand. This is known as *the counter-transference*, and it can be especially powerful if the analysand is projecting psychic energy onto the analyst that touches one of the analyst's own psychic wounds or complexes.

In this case, "if the analyst is not aware of his or her own shadow response, real harm can be done" as the analyst projects *his* shadow back onto the unsuspecting and vulnerable analysand (Woodman, 1995, p. 54). And what is more, the analyst's counter-transference may not always be a response to the analysand's projections. There may "just be something about" an analysand in the analyst's view that incites his counter-projection.

Just as the transference plays into relationship in general, so does counter-transference, particularly when one person holds more power in the relationship than the other does. When that is the case, we say the relationship is *asymmetrical*—as it is between a doctor and patient, lawyer and client, minister and parishioner—and, of course, teacher and student (Wiedemann, 1995).

Jung said that whenever there is an intense emotional relationship, there is the possibility of the creation of a special, psychically supercharged relational space that he called a *temenos*, or *sacred precinct* (Jung, 1992). Wherever there is the possibility of transformative transference/counter-transference dynamics (e.g., the consulting room or the classroom), there is also a potential *temenos*.

The physicist and Jungian Victor Mansfeld (Spiegelman & Mansfeld, 1996) even makes the intriguing claim that the emergence of a *temenos* in such places as the consulting room, the meditation hall, the bedroom, the field of battle, the classroom, and so on actually generates a psychophysical field that is conducive to certain paranormal and synchronistic phenomena (Spiegelman & Mansfeld, 1996). *Synchronicity,* by the way, is another term that is used a great deal by many people but with very few knowing that it was Carl Jung who gave it a name and tried to approach an understanding of how and why it comes about (Spiegelman & Mansfeld, 1996).

Jung's groundbreaking treatment of psychospiritual dynamics in the second half of life will be introduced in the next chapter, where we will examine some of the issues of midlife teachers in need of renewal.

PART TWO: EXERCISES IN
ARCHETYPAL REFLECTIVITY

1. Literature, cinema, myth, and religion provide many examples of great teachers. These characters range from the Buddha, Christ, Socrates, and Plato to Martin Luther King and Obi Won Kanobie. According to Jung, these figures exercise such power over us because they are archetypal symbols of the archetype of the teacher. What are some of the characteristics and qualities of these teachers? With these archetypal exemplars of the teacher in mind, consider your own path as a teacher. What of this archetypal vision of the teacher have you been able to realize in your own practice? What is left for you to realize? How might you go about doing this? What factors and forces, internal and external, might aid you in this?

Which might hinder you? In considering this, you might wish to consider psychological, institutional, cultural, ethical, and spiritual factors that are part of why you became a teacher, what has been influential in your history as a teacher, and how you see your future as a teacher.

2. When we think about various archetypes, certain characteristics of them come immediately to mind. For example, the archetype of the Young Hero causes us to think of such things as courage, strength, and adventurousness. But every archetype carries with it potential problems. Thus, in the Hero we also sometimes discern an innocence sometimes bordering on dangerous naivety, recklessness, and vanity.

    What are the positive sides of the archetype of the Teacher, especially as it inspired you to become a teacher? What are the problematic aspects of the Teacher archetype when, for example, the desire to nurture children, which is typically a part of this archetype, gets "off track" and teachers become so enmeshed with their students that those teachers' personal lives begin to suffer? We see this in teachers who spend too much time at home in school-related matters and don't leave enough time for their family? Being overly identified with any archetype can be a psychological problem. How can a teacher draw on the archetypal energy of the Teacher without being consumed by it?

3. Students are often quite intense in their feelings about their teachers. To many of us who stand in front of a classroom almost every day, it can be mystifying why students so often seem to be seeing and responding to us in either such extremely positive or negative terms, both of which seem unwarranted by the nature of the actual interaction so far. This is because the archetype of the teacher is so strong that it tends to touch students with a special immediacy at the archetypal level. Hence, students often see teachers through an archetypal lens. When we recall that every archetype has its light side and dark side, it is understandable why students often see their teacher in the hues of either great archetypal light or darkness.

    Share with your group of four or five classmates an instance of a time when you felt that a student was responding to you in an excessively deferential way and another in an excessively negative way. This was probably due to their archetypal transference onto you. Knowing that what was your response in each of these cases? How were they the same? How different? Knowing that both types of student responses to you may have been more about the archetype of the teacher than about you personally, what would have been different in your responses if you had been able to register their attitudes to you and frame them in archetypal terms?

4. The teacher is called upon to be many things to many students and fellow teachers. It is inevitable that a teacher may need to have various *personas* throughout the day. And as we saw in this chapter, it is not only inevitable

that a person has *personas* in order to harmoniously navigate the social world. Think of various *personas* that a teacher wears. Which ones do you consider natural and necessary for a teacher to wear? Explain why you think this is so. Also, talk about *personas* that teachers may put on that ultimately do not serve either them or their students in terms of their and their students' personal and intellectual development.

5. Try to think of times in your life as a teacher when the classroom seemed to be so charged with an electricity that it became a sacred space—a *temenos*. If you care to do so, share with your classmates this experience, speculating on what caused those special "transcendent" moments in the classroom. What was going on in the class? What were you teaching? How were you teaching it? How were the students relating to you? How were they relating to each other? In thinking about it now, does it tell you anything about how to create such a space in your future classroom teaching?

6. Jung insisted that we all have shadows. He also observed that we may cast our shadow inappropriately onto others. Can you think of a time when a student projected his shadow onto you? Were you aware at the time that this is what was happening and that it finally had nothing to do with *you* but had everything to do with the student's own shadow? If you were not thinking along these lines at the time, how might awareness of this have changed your response to the student and the effect the student's shadow-projections had upon you? Was there perhaps something in you that was eliciting the student's shadow? Conversely, think of a time that your negative feelings about a student may have arisen because you were projecting your shadow onto the student. How might knowledge of this have changed your feelings about the student and how you responded to him?

Chapter Three

Individuation and Vocation in the Second Half of Life

We have all heard of the midlife crisis. Many of you may have even passed through it or are passing through it now. What very few people know is that the idea of a midlife crisis is another psychological concept that originated with Jung.

Until Jung's model of lifespan development, virtually all other models of the individual's psychological evolution did not go very far past the first two decades of life. It was as if the individual experienced no substantial psychological development past late adolescence and that, if there was any development, it was just *quantitatively* different, just more of the same, but not *qualitatively* different enough to merit theorizing about it.

But what we might call "the 20-Max Model of Development" is counterintuitive. We all know from people whom we have observed, including ourselves if we are old enough, that the lifespan developmental challenges of a thirty-year-old are clearly and substantially different from those of a fifty-year-old, both of which in turn are different from those of a seventy-year-old.

This focus from Freud to Piaget on development in the first two decades of life was probably due to an overemphasis in psychological theory and in the society that sponsors it on *rational thought processes* (Piaget) and *sexual functioning* (Freud), both of which finally get largely established throughout adolescence. The ability to think rationally and to have a satisfying sexual life is undoubtedly important.

However, asked Jung, are there no other aspects of experience and other arenas of possibility that inspire the human being to move to even higher ground? There certainly are, said Jung, and they include such things as our longing for the aesthetically beautiful, our hunger for ethical purpose, our drive to be creative, and, above all, the passion in many of us for communication with the Transcendent.

45

Furthermore, Jung went on to query, is it not true that such things come into play with a special intensity and depth in the second half of life? To Jung it was clear that any adequate psychology could not leave human development stranded on the Island of 20-Max. It would have to help the individual understand and navigate those years past the *biological* zenith until middle age, and from there onward to the finish line of his life's *ethical* zenith.

Although a radical idea when Jung introduced it into psychological discourse in the opening years of the twentieth century, he was simply restating in psychological language what poets had long known and written about. Perhaps the most famous instance of this comes from Dante's *Divine Comedy*. Lamenting his own sense of disorientation and pain at about midlife, Dante wrote six centuries ago:

> Midway in our life's journey, I went astray
> From the straight road and woke to find myself
> Alone in a dark wood. How shall I say
> What wood that was! I never saw so drear,
> So rank, so arduous a wilderness!
> Its very memory gives a shape to fear. (1954, p. 28)

In less dire, more humorous tones, the great mythologist Joseph Campbell likened the midlife crisis to climbing up a very high ladder, finally getting to the top after great effort, looking around—and realizing that you climbed up the wrong wall!

Of course, it is not that one has really climbed up the wrong wall. One did what one was tasked by life to do in one's first half. It was the right wall at the time. It is simply that the developmental tasks are now different in the second half of life, generally from about forty years old on. The ladder has to be moved (or at least should be moved) to the balcony of the second floor so that one can reach the summit of the roof.

Some people understandably but mistakenly try to halt the developmental flow of biological and physical time by trying to remain "forever young." This can lead them into something as innocuous as a facelift or as risky as an extramarital affair with a much younger partner in order to maintain the illusion that one is still in his sexual prime.

For example, the NFL quarterback, having won two Super Bowl championships, continues to play past his peak in following seasons. He simply can't give up the thrill of the final-quarter touchdown he throws to snatch victory out of the jaws of defeat to the wild approval of an adoring stadium full of fans. But it is happening less and less often on the bottom-of-the-rankings team to which he has drifted over the eight years since his last Super Bowl victory when he was twenty-nine years old, and his team generally loses—final-quarter touchdown pass or not.

Another example is the fifty-year-old woman who has been dependent the past twenty-five years of her life upon her highly successful lawyer-husband as his trophy wife. However, she can see with increasingly painful clarity every morning as she looks in the mirror that the bloom went off some time ago and that there is nothing she can do to camouflage the withering effects of time any longer. No new cosmetic surgery, no regimen at an expensive weight-loss ranch can restore her to her gorgeous youth. Yet, she keeps scheduling surgeries and booking stays at the ranch in a futile attempt to look like her twenty-year-old daughter.

In Jungian psychology, we say that the quarterback and the wife are in the grips of the *Puer* and *Puella* Complexes, respectively. *Puer* is Latin for "boy" and *Puella* for "girl." The football player is a *Puer*, and the former beauty-pageant winner is a *Puella* because they will not relinquish the glory days of their youth in order to mature into something emotionally profound, ethically powerful, and of service to others in the second half of life. To do so would entail embracing the archetype of the Wise Elder. Moving toward a full embracing of this archetype in the man's and woman's life—not speedily but steadily and with a hard-won, unsentimental optimism and pragmatic idealism—is absolutely key to individuation in the second half of life.

Discovering the archetype of the Wise Elder and making it one's own in one's own way is what gives the second half of life renewed purpose and restored energy. This is quite necessary as one's biological system starts to slow down, libido to some degree lessens and in some instances simply goes away, children (if one has had any) leave home, and one becomes less and less driven by one's professional aspirations, which may have already peaked anyway. Personal, ego-oriented life projects informed by sexuality and social potency do not go away. But, in the best-case scenario from a Jungian perspective, they are increasingly in the service of the more refined imperatives of the new center of the personality in one's *transpersonal*, emerging, eternal Self. One becomes more efficacious in one's work at this period, not less so, if it is successfully negotiated, because one is now working under the pull of a higher vision, not a merely ego-oriented agenda.

However, this comes to pass only if the individual shakes off the *Puer* and *Puella* (keeping just enough of it to remain occasionally impish and sometimes even outrageous) and rises to his full stature as a Wise Elder. Then sex and personal power cease to be prime motivating factors, and one's eye turns to things that go beyond the appetites and strategies of the ego. The individual begins to search out more ethically nuanced and spiritually fertile existential territory upon which to move and act in his work and in his life in general. As William Butler Yeats wrote late in his life in his poem *Sailing to Byzantium*:

> That is no country for old men. The young
> In one another's arms, birds in the trees—
> Those dying generations—at their song,
> The salmon-falls, the mackerel-crowded seas,
> Fish, flesh, or fowl, commend all summer long
> Whatever is begotten, born, and dies.
> Caught in that sensual music all neglect
> Monuments of unageing intellect. (Yeats, 2004, p. 176)

Juxtaposed against the "sensual music" that proliferates in this stanza is the simple dignity of the single concluding line about "Monuments of unageing intellect." This must surely refer to those archetypal images, personages, stories, spiritual traditions, works of art, philosophical intuitions, and poetic visions that express universal truths that vary in form from culture to culture but are similar in substance. It is this archetypal knowledge that transforms a man or woman from simply being "elder" into being a "Wise Elder." The developmental task of the second half of life is to acquire more and more of this wisdom from decade to decade and to share it with one's culture. To do this is the search for the Holy Grail, the Hero's Journey, in the second half of life.

The Wise Elder serves the conservative function of anchoring his culture in exemplifying in his person the laws of the universe—what Buddhism calls "the Dharma." He also serves a radical function, which becomes clear when we consider the etymological origin of "radical" in the Latin word *radix*—or root. The Wise Elder calls his friends, family, coworkers, and youth back to those archetypal truths that are the *root* of psychological and cultural evolution. He, revolutionary, calls his culture forward, warning it off of fads and passing ideologies that lead to disorientation, illness, and even death.

Michael Geller (2001), in a fascinating study, *The Fate of America,* observes that the fact that contemporary American culture idolizes youth and ignores the elderly bodes very ill for the future of this country because it evidences its loss of contact with archetypal reality. It glorifies the *Puer* and *Puella* beyond all bounds and throws the Wise Elder on the garbage heap. The price of that is personal and cultural devolution into crass materialism, obsessive sexuality, and a fundamental unconcern with all people who have been shoved to the margins. This manifests itself in American culture as ageism. At the very stage in their lives when they have the most to offer the workforce by way of wisdom, our Wise Elders are cast aside to waste away on the margins.

This all boils down in many cases of "vocation," and it does so in two senses. First is the sense just discussed. The Elder is deprived of his vocation, or seen as less and less relevant within it, because of his age. The second sense is discovered by looking at the Latin root of "vocation" as a divine "calling" (*vocationem*) of the Wise Elder in the second half of his journey is to remind his people of his life, when, as a member of the workforce or not, he is archetypally called to restore his culture and even enable it to grow to even greater heights and depths.

Thus, it is not that the Wise Elder relinquishes contact with the world; rather, he is now called to engage in that contact with a nuanced sense of the psychological, social, and ethical perils and possibilities that are, past all the sexy news cycles of the day on cable news networks, what are truly at the heart of the affairs of the world. In his work he brings a seasoned perspective that makes him key in helping his organization see where to focus its time and resources by pointing out to his organization what is merely passing and what is solid. In whatever his activities may be, the Wise Elder does them fully aware that he is both an exemplar and a teacher of this core, ancient knowledge. Although he will probably never reap individual gain or fame from all of this, he knows that his thoughts and actions make a difference in his culture from the individual to the group level.

As the developmental psychologist Erik Erikson illustrated in his lifespan developmental model, knowing that one has made a positive difference in life is what alone brings a sense of completion and contentment as one passes through the last great developmental stage and approaches this life's finish line. It is what Erikson called a sense of psychological "integrity" as one transits through life's ultimate personal epoch. Without that sense, one ends one's life in existential "despair."

In sum, the person in the first half of life on the heroic journey pushes toward the consolidation of his ego-structure, the establishment of that ego-structure in the world of professional advancement, and, in many cases, the finding of a mate and the creation of a family, what Jung called its "personal aim." In the second half of life, however, the heroic journey transforms into what Jung called "the cultural aim" of the renewal of one's culture.

The heroic journey of the second half of life also entails the establishment of an "ego-Self axis." You will recall that we touched upon the notion of an ego-Self axis in our brief mention of Edward Edinger in chapter 2. Now is the time to say more of this concept that is so central to Jung's idea of individuation. In examining more closely the formation, maintenance, and development of this axis, we will concentrate on the idea of the Self since we have already looked in some depth at the much simpler idea of the ego in chapter 2.

As a procedural note, let us remember that Jung himself and his translators often (and rather confusingly) used the lower-case "s" in rendering into English the transpersonal self (*Das Selbst*). However, for the sake of clarity I will follow the practice of almost all Jungians today by using a capital "S" in the English rendering of *Das Selbst* to distinguish this Self from the mere egoic self (Jung, 1969b, p. 187).

MORE ON THE SELF

The Self is the repository of higher, timeless wisdom in the deepest realms of the individual psyche, even deeper than the merely personal, Freudian "subconscious," which contains memories of personal experiences that are so painful that is would be extremely difficult to go on functioning if one allowed oneself to be aware of them. The personal subconscious also contains individual needs, abilities, and drives that the individual has to repress in order to move harmoniously through the social order in which he lives.

The Self is different from the ego in many ways. The fundamental difference lies in the fact that it is not a product of our individual experiences but is inherently part of our nature as human beings. We are born with it, and the purpose of our life is to come into contact with it as clearly and creatively as we can. It is therefore, in theory, accessible to everyone—which is to say, it is *collective* and unites us as human beings.

However, because it lies even deeper than the subconscious and is not a product of our individual experiences but transcends them, it can never be fully known by merely ego-based consciousness—which is to say, it is more than merely *sub*-conscious. It is *un*-conscious. Hence Jung's signature phrase and most important idea: the *collective unconscious*. It goes beyond the *personal subconscious*, but it does not, as in Buddhist thought, *erase* the individual's identity but strives to bring the individual's personal identity into contact with his higher and deeper identity in his innermost, core Self. To do this is to establish an ego-Self axis.

The ego depends on syllogistic reasoning and personal experience. One's higher Self does not. This is not to say that the Self is *ir*-rational or oblivious to the individual's experience. It is to say that it is *trans*-rational and is thus uniquely positioned to make sense of that experience. It does not contradict reason; indeed, it often employs it, but it does go beyond mere reason into the realm of intuition. And what is more, it *can* be grasped, worked with, and assimilated through a deepening engagement with the symbols that it produces.

It is these "projected" archetypal images that constitute the lines of communication between ego and Self. As discussed earlier, archetypal images—especially in the form of dreams, art that one finds especially moving, experiences that have taken one outside of one's usual definition of oneself and have stayed with one throughout one's entire life, and sacred images/personages/narratives that impart meaning to one's life (whether or not they exist in the structure of an organized religion)—are the primary means of accessing and understanding one's Self.

The Self is who we fundamentally and perhaps even eternally *are*. The Self goes beyond our personal ego without erasing that identity but refining it in the crucible of experience—as in the poetry of William Blake, which exemplifies this process of moving from a state of innocence through experience to a consciousness that includes but transcends both and is therefore considered *trans*-personal.

Jung also saw this as the message of medieval and renaissance alchemy as practiced by the great religious alchemists of the time such as Michael Maier and Gerhardt Dorn. He felt that they were not concerned with the production of physical gold but rather the transformation of matter into spirit. He thus saw their work as symbolic of the process of individuation—the transmutation of the dross of the ego and subconscious into the gold of psychospiritually heightened consciousness.

Jung, a scientist as well as a mystic, borrowed a term from mathematics to describe this process of raising ego-bound psyche to the psychospiritual level of the Self. He called it the "transcendent function," as in exponential, logarithmic, and trigonometric functions, which go beyond mere linearity, as Self goes beyond ego. Honoring and claiming our essential identity as timeless beings, beyond the socially constructed identities that make up our ego, is the basic challenge of the second half of life. It is the ongoing dynamic of *individuation*.

When the ego moves into communication with the individual's Self, then his life becomes infinitely richer. The ego becomes spiritualized because it is touched with one's most profound "source." The Self becomes able to operate in and ethically affect one's life because it now has a mature ego to help it navigate the ordinary world of everyday business. Obviously, this gives one a renewed perspective on his work as a means of both summoning and spreading the influence of the Spirit. Establishing an "ego-Self" axis is the developmental passage that, if all goes well, typically begins in full force around midlife (Edinger, 1973, 1985).

Not everyone faces this passage bravely or productively. Some narcoticize themselves with a tedious but comforting regularity—what Thoreau called "a life of quiet desperation." Others lose themselves in practices and substances that for a little while allow them to maintain the illusion of endless youth. But these are both makeshifts, their shelf-life is very limited, and they do not lead to the psychospiritual profundity that individuation both requires of the individual and bestows upon him.

THE PERSONA AND THE SHADOW IN THE INDIVIDUATION PROCESS

According to Jung, the person who would earnestly pursue the path of individuation must "divest [the ego] of the false wrappings of the *persona*" (Jung, 1967b, p. 174). Jung does not mean here that the *persona* is bad. In fact, as we saw earlier, Jung insisted that *personas* are necessary in promoting social harmony. He simply meant to emphasize that individuation is a process that tends to accelerate as one ages and that this impacts one's *personas*.

For, as one ages, Jung felt, one should be focused much less on establishing personal identity or maneuvering for professional status, and should have his eyes more fixed on the prize of deepening wisdom and establishing more intimate ties with the Timeless. This naturally entails both a lessening of the number of *personas* one has in one's "social toolkit" and a cleansing of oneself from outright false *personas*. In like manner, individuation requires that one consciously integrate one's shadow to the maximum degree possible. As we saw in chapter 2, this requires considerable effort, not a little pain, and a skillful use of one's shadowy side as a means of healthy empowerment in effecting positive change in the world—largely through one's work.

Moreover, since individuation entails that one has become whole— integrating and reconciling both light and dark in oneself into the form a mature, *completed* being who can use the totality of who he naturally is and who he has become in life to work for the good—it is by definition crucial that one successfully confront and channel one's shadow in the second half of life. Confronting one's shadow, as well as the other developmental tasks that one must come to grips with in the second half of life (not least of which is one's dwindling physical strength and attractiveness as one moves into the final decades), is difficult work, not for the faint of heart. Nevertheless, it is worth it, bringing peace, fulfillment, and the fortitude to face one's aging and death with courage and hope. Wrote Jung:

> So far as we can make out, *individuation* is a natural phenomenon, and in a way an inescapable goal, which we have reason to call *good for us*, because it liberates us from the otherwise insoluble conflict of opposites (at least to a noticeable degree). It is not invented by man, but Nature herself produces its archetypal image. Thus the credo "in the end all shall be well" is not without its psychic foundation. (Jung, 1977, p. 727)

Furthermore, individuation is not only *possible* for everyone by virtue of their being human beings, but it is also *necessary* for everyone to constantly be striving for higher degrees of individuation—a strengthening and maturing of the ego-Self axis, an ever more nuanced conversation between one's social self in the form of the ego and one's timeless self in the form of the Self. An added advantage of this in our postmodern, radically pluralistic times is that individuation, although essentially a spiritual endeavor, is quite free of specific religious systems or attachments. It is also free of socioeconomic status, professional position, level of education, or any of the other social distinctions that are all important in the everyday world of the ego, but quite irrelevant in the timeless world of spirit. Thus Jung reassures us that the possibility of psychic development . . . is not reserved for specially gifted individuals. In other words, in order to undergo a far-reaching psychological development, neither outstanding intelligence nor any other talent is necessary, since in this development moral qualities can make up for intellectual shortcomings. It must not on any account be imagined that the treatment consists in grafting upon people's minds general formulas and complicated doctrines. There is no question of that. Each can take what he needs, in his own way and in his own language. (Jung, 1967b, p. 116)

THE SYMBOL IN INDIVIDUATION

As we have seen throughout this book, archetypes express themselves in a different language from that used in merely logical analyses and propositional assertions. They must speak to us in the higher language of symbols, those "time-bound expressions of timeless realities" (Henderson, 1984, p. 249). Archetypal symbols—especially in dreams, religion, and art—are not of a lower order of reality—as our "I-have-to-see-it-to-believe it," commodity-obsessed society would have us believe. Indeed, they are of a higher order because they point *beyond* us, and at the same time *within* us, to transcendent truths.

With such a premium placed on the symbolic realm, it should not be surprising that Jung offered many definitions of what a symbol is. One of the simplest and most famous of these is that a symbol is "the best possible expression for something that cannot be expressed otherwise than by a more or less close analogy" (*CW* 6, par. 3, n. 44). Symbols go beyond mere reason because they offer the "the best possible expression for a complex fact not yet clearly apprehended by consciousness" (*CW* 8, par. 148).

A mere concept is limited because, being merely rational, it cannot fully grasp the infinitely complex emotional ground from which all our mentally processes primally arise nor the transcendent heights to which our spiritual aspirations reach. Symbols can. Thus, the symbol, Jung declared, is "the primitive exponent of the unconscious, but at the same time an idea that corresponds to the highest intuition of the conscious mind" (*CW* 18, par. 44). Thus, the Freudian approach, which merely *analyzes* a symbol (and does so strictly within the limitations of the sexual impulse) is, although useful at times, often quite limited.

Symbols express our entire being. That is why we must authentically *interact* with our symbols in dreams, art, myth, and religion if we are to be authentically and productively *changed* by them in our totality. There are many techniques in Jungian psychology for doing this. One technique, of course, is common to all forms of depth psychology: dream analysis. Another is the production and appreciation of art. Another is bringing greater attention to the symbols that might make up one's faith tradition but that one has taken for granted. Yet another is examining and reframing one's life in terms of archetypal images, characters, and narratives—"re-narrativizing" one's life. Yet another is *active imagination.*

In active imagination, the analysand, in the waking state, allows herself to continue with an image or theme of a particular dream, fantasy, or simply one's own invention to see where it might lead. Jung wrote:

> Continuous conscious realization of unconscious fantasies, together with active participation in the fantastic events, has, as I have witnessed in a very large number of cases, the effect firstly of extending the conscious horizon by the inclusion of numerous unconscious contents; secondly of gradually diminishing the dominant influence of the unconscious; and thirdly of bringing about a change of personality. (Jung, 1967b, p. 219)

Naturally, this does not imply that we must *act out* on the images from our dream life—although active imagination may lead to images, emotions, and thoughts that might lead us to making changes in our lives. Indeed, changing one's life so that it can become happier and more creative in the daily world is a central purpose of active imagination. In this way, active imagination emerges as a powerful tool in creating an ego-Self axis—a wedding of the ageless wisdom of the unconscious mind with the practical efficacy of the conscious mind.

When this happens, the ego is guided by the Spirit while the Spirit manifests itself pragmatically in the ego. And it cannot be stressed too much that this synergy of ego and Self keeps the ego from shriveling up for lack of spiritual nutrition and keeps the Spirit from leading the individual into wildly impractical and even dangerous ventures.

Denied the life-giving flow from the archetypal realm into a person or culture, that person or culture begins to perish for lack of purpose and passion. In our often crassly materialistic culture, this *asymbolism* leads to a sense of meaninglessness and despair, which people vainly try to fill up with everything from extreme sports to irresponsible sex, from the glorification of greed to the delusions induced by drugs. In a conversation with a group of British psychiatrists, Jung emphasized this cultural malady—the meaninglessness that is both produced and reflected in the lack of compelling symbols that provide ethical and spiritual direction to a culture. "Now we have no symbolic life," he sadly observed,

> and we are all badly in need of the symbolic life. Only the symbolic life can express the soul—the daily need of the soul, mind you! And because people have no such thing, they can never step out of this mill—this awful, grinding,

banal life in which they are "nothing but." . . . [T]here is no symbolic existence in which I am something else, in which I am fulfilling my role, my role as one of the actors in the divine drama of life. . . . That gives the only meaning to human life. That gives peace, when people feel that they are living the symbolic life, that they are actors in the divine drama. . . . [E]verything else is banal and you can dismiss it. (Jung, 1977, pp. 274–275)

In sum, the ego's conscious mind can grasp, and be grasped by, the Self by means of archetypal symbols, which function as a kind of bridge between ego and Self. The individuating life then becomes an ongoing communication between the reality of our everyday lives and the realm of the Spirit. We each, in our own way, become a unique embodiment of the ego-Self axis, and in this we find something worth living for and ways of acting with conviction and compassion in the world.

INDIVIDUATION AS A "MYSTERIUM CONIUNCTIONIS"[1]

As we have seen, individuation entails the unification of all sorts of opposites as an overarching task. After all, individuation is maturity, and maturity requires looking at both sides of things, taking the best from both, and reconciling the dialectical tension in the form of a higher synthesis. This synthesis is not to be understood merely as some sort of compromise between the two extremes although compromise may be a part of what is going on. Rather, the synthesis is fundamentally a new creation, a "third," as Jung often called it, that not only combines the best of two opposing things but goes beyond them in the form of a unifying symbol—like a child who so far outshines her parents' best gifts and fondest expectations that they can only look at her in stunned admiration.

Jung called this ability to generate a higher third out of paired opposites "*the transcendent function*" (Jung, 1967b, p. 80). He also called it a *coincidentia oppositorum*—that is, opposites coming together—(Jung, 1967a, p. 368), or a *unio mystica*—a mystical union (Jung, 1967a, p. 287). All of these terms suggest that this process is always something of a mystery, just as the cosmic operation of the *Tao* in the intercourse of *yin* and *yang* is a mystery. *Tertium non datur*—"the third is not given"—as one of Jung's favorite Latin saying goes, implying the enigma of growth itself. The force-fields generated by the tug-and-pull of paired opposites are the very womb out of which all new life—physical and psychic—proceeds, but we ultimately are quite in the dark about how this actually happens.

The genius of Eastern philosophy and religion—and an important part of the Buddha's message—is the recognition that everything contains the possibility of turning into its opposite. Therefore, the project of finding balance, peace, and creativity in a transcendent "third" is of the greatest importance psychically and morally:

> Unfortunately, our Western mind . . . has never yet devised a concept, nor even a name for the *union of opposites through the middle path*, that most fundamental item of inward experience, which could respectably be set against the Chinese concept of Tao. It is at once the most individual fact and the most universal, the most legitimate fulfillment of the meaning of the individual's life. (Jung, 1967b, p. 205).

Yet we need not reach for such philosophical heights to understand the homespun truth that Jung was trying to convey. For it is a commonsense fact that the firmest alliances may turn into the bitterest contentions; the healthiest regimen, taken too far, inevitably breeds some sort of pathology by and by; and even the most passionate idealism (indeed, *especially* the most passionate idealism) may turn into resigned realism at best and cynicism at worst. The principle that things turn into their opposites given enough time is called *enantiodromia*. It has important therapeutic implications.

> The tendency to separate the opposites as much as possible and to strive for singleness of meaning is absolutely necessary for clarity of consciousness, since discrimination is of its essence. But when separation is carried so far that the complementary opposite is lost sight of, and the blackness of the whiteness, the evil of the good, the depth of the heights, and so on, is no longer seen, the result is one-sidedness, which is then compensated from the unconscious without our help. The counterbalancing is even done against our will, which in consequence must become more and more fanatical until it brings about a catastrophic enantiodromia. Wisdom never forgets that all things have two sides. (Jung, 1970c, pp. 333–334)

The feeling type must learn not only to *have* deep values that inform her every decision but must *examine* them, too; otherwise, there will be an *enantiodromia* and her values may lead her into awkward, even unethical, commitments that a bit of hard-headed analysis could have avoided. And the intuitive type would do well not only to anticipate the future but also to focus more fully on present constraints and conditions, lest the reality of the present stealthily undermine the dreams of the future by means of *enantiodromia*.

If reality is dialectical, then it follows that the archetypes should also be dialectical. Thus, the archetype of the great nurturing mother has its dark flipside—the archetype of the great devouring mother. The archetype of the wise old man has as his dialectical opposite the ossified old tyrant. In myth and fairytale, the fair visage of the lovely virgin is sometimes just a mask worn by the destructive seductress, and even a prince can be a frog. As Alice discovered in Wonderland, just step through the mirror and everything becomes its reverse. To come into living contact with the realm of archetypes, therefore, is to recognize that one is both light and dark and that one contains every good and evil human potential. The purpose of individuation is to bring all of this together in advancing one's own psychospiritual growth and being of greater service to one's fellow beings. Without this, the second half of life is an exercise in futility, ending only in the grave. With it, one's life and work in the second half of life spiral upward in a sense of meaningful labor and, for many people as they approach the end of this mortal race, the hope of something beyond.

PART TWO: EXERCISES IN ARCHETYPAL REFLECTIVITY

1. As teachers we know that there is a decreasing appreciation of the heroic work that we do every day in the classroom, an increasing criticism of us by politicians from both the liberal and conservative camps, and a resulting focus on standardizing of education in a way that would take the joy, spontaneity, and creativity out of schooling for both us and our students. This causes many teachers to despair of their work and leave teaching. How might you employ what you have learned in this book to "reframe" or "re-narrativize" your work as a teacher that will help you recapture your sense of purpose and at the same time help resist as much as possible the corporate agendas that are being imposed upon education?

2. There are many movies that focus on the midlife transition—*Lost in Translation, American Beauty, Falling Down, Young Adult, Thelma and Louise, About a Boy, The Weather Man*, just to name a few. With your class, do a Google search of "midlife crisis movies" to find one that you would all like to watch. After, discuss how the movie exhibited how the protagonist either did or did not negotiate the transition well. Also, did the movie evidence archetypal narratives/characters/images that one might associate with the midlife transition?

3. How can what you have read in this book help you deal with a midlife crisis regarding your work as a teacher? If you are still too young to have confronted this challenge, how do you feel you might do so in the future, having learned about this crisis in archetypal terms in this book? If you are presently experiencing such a transition, does what you have read in this book give you some ideas about how to handle it effectively or help you understand better why what you *have done already* has worked well?

If you have passed through this crisis, how has your reading of this book
perhaps helped you understand the ways in which you perhaps did or
didn't handle that transition as creatively as possible?

NOTE

1 Parts of the following section are drawn from Cliff's 2005 work *Jung and
Education: Elements of an Archetypal Pedagogy,* published by Rowman & Littlefield
Press.

REFERENCES

Adams, M. (1996). *The multicultural imagination: "Race," color, and the uncon-
scious.* London: Routledge.
Bernstein, H. (1989). The courage to try: Self-esteem and learning. In K. Field, B.
Cohler, and G. Wool (Eds.). *Learning and education: Psychoanalytic perspectives*
(pp. 143–157). Madison, Connecticut: International Universities Press, Inc.
Block, A. (1997) *I'm only bleeding: Education as the practice of social violence
against children.* New York: Peter Lang.
Britzman, D. (2011). *Freud and education.* London: Routledge.
Brown, J., Collins, A. and Duguid, O. (1988). Situated cognition and the culture of
learning. *Educational Researcher, 18*(32–42).
Buber, M. (1985). *Between man and man.* New York: Scribners.
Buber, M. (1965). *I and thou.* New York: Vintage.
Campbell, J. (1949). *The hero with a thousand faces.* Princeton, New Jersey: Princ-
eton University Press.
Cohler, B. (1989). Psychoanalysis and education: Motive, meaning, and self. In K.
Field, B. Cohler, and G. Wool (Eds.), *Learning and education: Psychoanalytic per-
spectives* (pp. 11–84). Madison, Connecticut: International Universities Press, Inc.
Conger, J., and Galambos, J. (1997). *Adolescence and youth: Psychological develop-
ment in a changing world.* New York: Longman.
Cornett, C. (1998). *The soul of psychotherapy: Recapturing the spiritual dimension
in therapeutic encounter.* New York: The Free Press.
Cremin, L. (1988). *American education: The metropolitan experience:* New York:
Harper and Row.
Dante. (1954). *The inferno.* (Translated by John Ciardi). New York: Signet Classics.
Dewey, J. (1916). *Democracy and education.* New York: Macmillan.
Edinger, E. (1973). *Ego and archetype: Individuation and the religious function of the
psyche.* Baltimore: Penguin Press.
Eisner, E. (1985). *The educational imagination: On the design and evaluation of
school programs* (New York: Macmillan, 1985)
Erikson, E. (1997). *The life cycle completed.* New York: W.W. Norton.
Fordham, M. (1996). In S. Shamdasani (Ed.), *Analyst-patient interaction: Collected
papers on technique.* London: Routledge.

Field, K., Cohler, B., and Wool, G. (Eds.). (1989). *Learning and education: Psychoanalytic perspectives*. Madison, Connecticut: International Universities Press, Inc.

Frankl, V. (1967) *Man's search for meaning* (New York: Washington Square Press).

Frazer, J. (1935). *The golden bough: a study in magic and religion*. New York: The Macmillan Company.

Freire, P. (1970). *The pedagogy of the oppressed*. New York: Seabury Press.

Freud, S. (1990). The dynamics of transference. In A. Esman (Ed.), *Essential papers on transference* (pp. 28–36). New York: New York University Press.

Freud, S. (1970). *A general introduction to psycho-analysis*. New York: Simon and Schuster.

Frey-Rohn, L. (1974). *From Freud to Jung: A comparative study of the psychology of the unconscious*. New York: G. P. Putnam's Sons.

Gellert, M. (2001). *The fate of America: An inquiry into national character*. Washington, D.C.: Brassey's, Inc.

Goffman, E. (1997). *The Goffman reader*. C. Lemert, and A. Branaman (Eds.). London: Blackwell.

Greenson, R. (1990). The working alliance and the transference neurosis. In A. Esman (Ed.). *Essential papers on transference* (pp. 150–171). New York: New York University Press.

Henderson, J. (1984). The Jungian interpretation of history and its educational implications. In R. Papadopoulos and G. Saayman (Eds.). *Jung in modern perspective: The master and his legacy* (pp. 245–255). Lindfield, Australia: Unity Press.

Jung, C. (1992). *The psychology of the transference*. Princeton, New Jersey: Princeton University Press.

Jung, C.G. (1977). *The symbolic life* (R. F. C. Hull, Trans.). (Volume 18 in the *Collected Works*). Princeton, New Jersey: Princeton University Press.

Jung, C.G. (1971). *Psychological types* (R. F. C. Hull, Trans.). (Volume 6 in the *Collected Works*). Princeton, New Jersey: Princeton University Press.

Jung, C.G. (1970a). *Civilization in transition* (R. F. C. Hull, Trans.). (Volume 10 in the *Collected Works*). Princeton, New Jersey: Princeton University Press.

Jung, C.G. (1970b). *Psychology and religion: West and East* (R. F. C. Hull, Trans.). (Volume 11 in the *Collected Works*). Princeton, New Jersey: Princeton University Press.

Jung, C.G. (1970c). *Mysterium coniunctionis* (R. F. C. Hull, Trans.). (Volume 14 in the *Collected Works*). Princeton, New Jersey: Princeton University Press.

Jung, C.G. (1969a). *The structure and dynamics of the psyche* (R. F. C. Hull, Trans.). (Volume 8 in the *Collected Works*). Princeton, New Jersey: Princeton University Press.

Jung, C.G. (1969b). *The archetypes and the collective unconscious* (R. F. C. Hull, Trans.). (Volume 9.1 in the *Collected Works*). Princeton, New Jersey: Princeton University Press.

Jung, C.G. (1969c). *Aion: Researches into the phenomenology of the self* (R. F. C. Hull, Trans.). (Volume 9.2 in the *Collected Works*). Princeton, New Jersey: Princeton University Press.

Jung, C.G. (1968a). *Psychology and alchemy* (R. F. C. Hull, Trans.). (Volume 12 in the *Collected Works*). Princeton, New Jersey: Princeton University Press.

Jung, C.G. (1968b). *Alchemical studies* (R. F. C. Hull, Trans.). (Volume 13 in the *Collected Works*). Princeton, New Jersey: Princeton University Press.

Jung, C.G. (1967a). *Symbols of transformation: Analysis of the prelude to a case of schizophrenia* (R. F. C. Hull, Trans.). (Volume 5 in the *Collected Works*). Princeton, New Jersey: Princeton University Press.

Jung, C.G. (1967b). *Two essays on analytical psychology* (Volume 7 in the *Collected Works*). (R. F. C. Hull, Trans.). Princeton, New Jersey: Princeton University Press.

Jung, C.G. (1966a). *The spirit in man, art, and literature* (R. F. C. Hull, Trans.). (Volume 15 in the *Collected Works*). Princeton, New Jersey: Princeton University Press.

Jung, C.G. (1966b). *The practice of psychotherapy: Essays on the psychology of the transference and other subjects* (R. F. C. Hull, Trans.). (Volume 16 in the *Collected Works*). Princeton, New Jersey: Princeton University Press.

Jung, C.G. (1954). *The development of personality: Papers on child psychology, education, and related subjects* (R. F. C. Hull, Trans.). (Volume 17 in the *Collected Works*). Princeton, New Jersey: Princeton University Press.

Knox, J. (1998). Transference and countertransference. In I. Alister and C. Hauke (Eds.), *Contemporary Jungian analysis: Post-Jungian perspectives from the society of analytic psychology* (pp. 73–84). London: Routledge.

Kohut, H. (1978). *The search for self: Selected writings of Heinz Kohut: 1950–1978.* P. Ornstein (Ed.). Madison, CT: International Universities Press.

Kuhn, T. (1970). *The structure of scientific revolutions.* Chicago: University of Chicago Press.

Main, R. (2004). *The rupture of time: Synchronicity and Jung's critique of modern Western culture.* New York: Brunner-Routledge.

Maslow, A. (1968). *Toward a psychology of being* (2nd edition). Princeton, New Jersey: D. Van Nostrand.

Mayes, C. (2017). *Teaching and learning for wholeness: The Role of archetypes in educational processes.* Lanham, Maryland: Rowman and Littlefield Press.

Mayes, C. (2016). *An introduction to the* Collected Works *of C.G. Jung: Psyche as spirit.* Lanham, Maryland: Rowman & Littlefield Press.

Mayes, C. (2009). *The hero's journey in teaching and learning: A study in Jungian pedagogy.* Madison, Wisconsin: Atwood.

Mayes, C. (2007). *Inside education: Depth psychology in teaching and learning.* Madison, Wisconsin: Atwood.

Mayes, C. (2005). The teacher as shaman. *Journal of Curriculum Studies, 37*(3), 329–348.

Mayes, C. (2004) *Teaching Mysteries: Foundations of a spiritual pedagogy* (Lanham, Maryland: University Press of America).

Mayes, C. (2002). Personal and archetypal aspects of transference and countertransference in the classroom. *Encounter: Education for Meaning and Social Justice, 15*(2), 34–49.

Pintrich, P., Marx, R., & Boyle, R. (1993). Beyond cold conceptual change: The role of motivational beliefs and classroom contextual factors in the process of conceptual change. *Review of Educational Research, 63,* 167–199

Neumann, E. (1954). *The origins and history of consciousness* (vol. 1). New York: Harper Brothers.

Salzberger-Wittenberg, I. (1989). *The emotional experience of learning and teaching.* London: Routledge and Kegan Paul.

Shamdasani, S. (2003). *Jung and the making of modern psychology: The dream of a science.* Cambridge, U.K.: Cambridge University Press.

Spiegelman, J. and Mansfeld, V. (1996). On the physics and psychology of the transference as an interactive field. In J. Spiegelman (Ed.), *Psychotherapy as a mutual process* (pp. 183–206). Tempe, Arizona: New Falcon Publications.

Tillich, P. (1956). *The essential Tillich.* New York: Macmillan Publishing Co.

Wiedemann, F. (1995). Mother, father, teacher, sister: Transference/countertransference with women in the first stage of animus development. In N. Schwartz-Salant & M. Stein (Eds.). *Transference/countertransference* (pp. 175–190). Wilmette, Illinois: Chiron Publications.

Winnicott, D.W. (1988) *Psychoanalytic explorations.* In D.W. Winnicott, R. Shepherd, and M. Davis (Eds.). Cambridge, Massachusetts: Harvard University Press.

Woodman, M. (1995). Transference and countertransference in analysis dealing with eating disorders. In N. Schwartz-Salant and M. Stein (Eds.), *Transference/countertransference* (pp. 53–66). Wilmette, Illinois: Chiron Publications.

Yeats, W.B. (2004). *The collected poetry of William Butler Yeats.* New York: Vintage.

Chapter Four

Individuation, the "Vocatus," and Teaching

Teaching is more than a noble profession. It is a vocation, a calling. The teacher is the most important person in any civilization, as on him (her) depends the molding of the nation. There are not many born teachers, but there are those who love teaching, find it meaningful, and there are those who enter it as an occupation.

Teaching Is a Vocation—A Calling, By "Teacher Randall butsingh, worldpress, 1962"—1962

I used to think teaching was a job. And then I thought it was a profession. Now I'm of the opinion that it's a calling. It's a very noble calling. It brings excitement. It brings despair. Why, I cannot think of any other calling which is so demanding. I love it. It makes me who I am.

Ron L., fifth-grade teacher

Central to the theme of Jung's concept of vocation and call is individuation. Individuation is the idea that there is a way to recognize yourself that is ideal. It is the realization of this ideal identity along a path that leads to an expression of your authentic self. Thus, individuation is the process that the psyche takes in search of the Soul or Self. It is a quest for ultimate meaning for both numinous and physical metanoia.

An important part of the individuation process is consciousness. The development of the ego consciousness (growing up) interrupts a sense of wholeness we have as children. In addition to consciousness, there is the sense of individuation being about returning to that state of wholeness, returning to the stream of life from which we came prior to birth. Developing consciousness or an ego state fragments you from your life—it moves you from the source of life. You are not as connected to the source as you are when you are in an unconscious state.

One sees this most often in children. Children have not only a physical but a spiritual energy, and the more they mature the more it tends to diminish. There is a time, and teachers see this, where children exist in a state of grace not needing to understand the meaning and purpose of life. Living is enough. Just being alive is purposeful. One doesn't need to question existence. But for most of us, that does not last indefinitely. We have a sense of moving from a state of simply being in the world to one where there are questions like, "is being alive worthwhile" or "why am I alive?" Indeed, we all have consciousness, and it comes at a price; it separates us from what Jung called the collective unconscious.

Another key definition that must be explored is the concept of "meaning." Both for Jung and his individuation process, the degree that your life is meaningful is a good test of where you stand in that process. Hence, living a meaningful life is living an individuated one. Now there's a distinction between what is meaningful and what is purposeful. In the first, your experience is meaningful— you experience your life as meaningful. Now what would be the opposite? An absence of meaning. Sometimes in your life, you may have felt that you simply were going through the motions. Or you're in certain relationships or pursuing certain projects but your mind asks, why? There is a sense of doubt—an absence of meaning or an absence of joy in what you're doing.

The important point is that individuation is an increased meaning for life. It has little to do with achievements or how grand one thinks one is—an individuated person can lead a very simple life but her experience would be extremely meaningful. So individuation is a journey to meaning. Where in my life am I taken seriously? Where in my life do I experience meaning? Where do I feel alive?

Let me give you an example: based on our studies, the more one becomes blended in with the crowd, the more one will be ensconced in having the security that a regular paycheck, a routinized curriculum, and friends provide. But there may come a time when we recognize that we are trapped in an economic reality. With that recognition, money may come to be seen as only pieces of paper and metal which are useful but not important in any ultimate sense. Each of us has an economic task and an economic wounding. For some stay-at-home parents who forewent outside employment in order to solely focus on nurturing their families, they may feel denied some empowerment or economic freedom. Others (especially sole economic providers for their families), laden with dental bills and college tuitions, may feel as time goes on that their economic tasks (jobs) are straight jackets — leashed and constrained by a never-ending collar. I (Mark) remember a day that I left the Pentagon after giving several top-level briefings, driving through Washington DC traffic, arriving home, and not knowing how I got there. I was sleepwalking through my life at age thirty-seven. At the top of my professional game, but sleepwalking! Living the dream, as my plumber says, but hardly living.

To meet economic realities, we must work—often for the rest of our lives. But there is another path that we've been talking about which is seldom one of security and comfort. You must leave home psychologically, and it will change you and all who come in contact with if you choose to walk this path. Carl Jung intimated that there was a huge difference between a job to meet economic demands and a vocation that awakens us as part of the individuation process. He pointed to both the Christ and the Buddha as people who followed in the footsteps that the numinous directed. In other words, they took up the cup passed on to them by God—the *vocatus* (Latin for "calling"). They followed their call.

A vocation chooses us. Our choice is in how we respond. In order to live numinously and live out your purpose, you must recognize it and take the steps toward the path. Recall Jonah from the biblical Old Testament. He chose not to listen to the calling from God to preach to the people of Nineveh because he believed that it would be a waste of time. Ultimately, Yahweh would spare them. So what was the use? Thus, Jonah rejected the call and took a boat to a place where he assumed that he could carry on his life free from God's interference.

But it becomes clear that this task was more about Jonah than Nineveh alone. It is about the making of a person who would see from the Deity's perspective and find purpose in life. As soon as he enters the boat, a tempest comes up and threatens all lives aboard the ship. Everyone is praying to their gods for help, all except Jonah. He is in the middle of the ship fast asleep! You see the issue? He is asleep—not psychologically awakened or on his path to awakening. He's in a sports car going seventy miles an hour in escape mode near Baltimore, like I felt during home from the Pentagon.

The ship master comes to him and does Jonah a profound favor. He asks him a question that every psychologist and friend should be asking those going through difficult times: "what meanest thou O Sleeper? Arise, call upon thy God " (KJV); in other words, look at your dreams, ask your friends, plea to the numinous for insight so that you may grow and save us and yourself.

Then, after a sequence of synchronicities, the lot of determination falls upon Jonah. "Who are you that your God should be so angry with us? they ask. And for the first time in this Hero's journey, Jonah recognizes that he is the problem. "I am Hebrew." he says and tells them the rest of the story. Jonah also recognizes and becomes clear on what must be done. He should be thrown into the water (symbolic for the unconscious, baptism, and death) and the seas would calm. Despite the sailors' protests, they eventually toss him in. The tempest is pacified.

Jonah is on a journey now. God has a plan for Jonah to become more individuated, more aware of the Self. A Leviathan. A whale. A living cave swallows up Jonah and he is given three days in the belly to consider himself and his life. As Carl Jung put its "He who looks outside dreams. He looks within awakens." What pain—what ugliness—what torture to be in the belly of the whale and not know whether or not one would be forgiven or saved? Jonah tires. "Kill me," he pleads. "Forgive me," he begs. He looks inward and recognizes the voice of God.

One way of looking at this journey is to observe that the psyche presents us with two large questions—one" one for each of the two halves of our lives. The question of the first half is "What is the world asking of me?" and that of the second is "What, now, does the soul ask of me?" Take the Call, the Hebrew God directs. Jonah accepts the call for his second half of life. But he is still somewhat blind to what God is doing! Nevertheless, he is forced to ask some tough questions of himself while in the body of darkness. Here are some of the questions he may have asked and answered (or at least began to answer):

What is my shadow and how can I make it known?
What is my myth?
What is my vocation?
What are my spiritual points of reference?
What fiction shall be my truth?
What is my obligation to the world?
What's this death business?
What and who supports me?
What matters in the end?

Upon being vomited out of the fish's belly, he goes to Nineveh and the people there accept his message and repent of their sins. Jonah is now displeased with God because the city was spared. Jonah said that he knew that God was going to spare them even before boarding the ship for Tarshish. Yet this entire hero's journey was partially for Jonah's benefit as well. For as the town repented, God caused a giant gourd to grow in the desert under which Jonah could take respite. What great shade it must have offered from the relentless sun. Once Jonah became used to it, God caused a worm to destroy the gourd. Jonah was greatly saddened. So God stopped to explain that Jonah should imagine the love that God has for the people of Nineveh compared to Jonah's love for the gourd. No comparison. Opening your eyes and hearing God or the "Self" is what prods us along the road less traveled. In the case of Jonah, he ignored the prodding at the risk of rendering his life devoid of meaning, an empty journey always escaping from the Call.

Jungian analyst James Hollis in his work on Jung and the Middle Passage examines Christ's life similarly. Analyzing Kazantzakis's novel *The Last Temptation of Christ*, he points out that like Jonah, Jesus of Nazareth may have wanted to escape the Call of becoming the Christ:

[Jesus in the novel] merely wishes to be like his father, a carpenter who makes crosses for the Roman authorities. He wants to marry Mary Magdalene, live in the suburbs, drive a sports version of the camel, and have 2.2 children. The voice within, the vocatus, calls him to a different place. His last temptation, experiencing loneliness and abandonment by his father, is to renounce his calling and become an ordinary person. When he imagines his life that way, he realizes he would have betrayed himself by betraying his individuation. In saying yes to his vocatus, Jesus becomes the Christ. So Jung said that the proper imitation Christi was not to live like the Nazarene of old, but to live one's individuation, one's vocation as fully as Jesus lived the Christ. (Hollis, 73)

The final story I want to share with you does not come from sacred history but rather from American literature. It demonstrates that the individuation process is a series of turnings along long-winding yellow-brick roads. Frank L. Baum, who wrote a series of stories about Dorothy and her mischievous dog, Toto, had one narrative come to the silver screen—the 1938 version of *The Wizard of Oz*. This coming-of age tale pits childhood against the adult world where the protagonist finds that it is simply a shifting of perspective due to various experiences and relationships that help her grow to find that there is "no place like home." But the story is more than that—whether Baum knew it or not, his narrative struck a chord with a nation in crisis (the Great Depression and the onset of World War II) and provided a story for America's coming of age as a super power. As a historian, I am drawn to articulate how the story simultaneously weaved itself into and emanated from the American psyche. I also want to demonstrate how, like most great narratives, the story has connections to the overall human condition as well. It is a heroine's journey to individuation.

The movie version of Oz begins in a dark place—Kansas and 1930s Depression Dustbowl America. Dorthey Gale, an orphan, and her dog (a trickster) get into a lot of trouble when the animal gets into the flower (weed) bed of a local grouchy spinster. The sheriff comes to take away the dog, and Dorothy responds in the only way she sees possible—through flight. And her journey to enlightenment begins. She starts on a path to a place over the rainbow and finds that she is a technicolor "good witch" in training. She is taught by the archetypes of intelligence (Scarecrow), emotion (Tinman), and courage (Lion) to first face her shadow (Wicked Witch) and acknowledge it. Through a series of trials and intrigues and with the help of the Good Witch (Mother archetype) and a brush with death, Dorothy finally finds that if she looks inside, she will at any given time find her way home. She is now free to return home and bring the treasure with her, which is the knowledge that "there is no place like home." The movie ends there inspiring the viewer to recognize that one should look to self, home, and family for answers to harmful witches of the world. Moreover, it says that to be truly heroic, we must take a step out of the ordinary and be prepared to never be the same.

Whether discussing sacred history or popular culture, many stories as Joseph Campbell demonstrated in his book *Hero with a Thousand Faces* follow a path of a search for meaning and credibility around the theme of individuation. The story usually begins with a "calling," followed by a denial of the call and then many adventures culminating with a visit to the belly of the whale—where the "called one" finally accepts the gods, demands to finish the journey. Once out of the whale or dark place, the hero takes up the quests with a little help from friends and becomes knighted or awarded the kingdom. All that the hero learns is brought back to home where he or she may be crowned king/queen of the land. Such is the individuation process. The hero's journey is an archetypal constellate (much in the way that a complex forms)—that is several archetypes joining together in a plot of finding meaning in the first and second parts of life. Jonah, Christ, and Dorothy have stories that we can identify with as we live in similar plots at various times in our own lives.

So how does a teacher find meaning during a period of chronic fatigue or significant stress—from issues such as parents, assessments, low pay, and little encouragement from administrators? As one is being called to go deeper into one's psyche (*psyche* is Greek for "soul"), to start the individuation journey, we recommend gaining a good handle on how you as a person take in information and then process it.

The best Jungian tools for determining typology are the pairing up of an instrument such as the Meyers-Briggs Type Indicator (MBTI) with a certified type practitioner to get at your code. The MBTI is not a test by any means. It does not measure traits, provide you with a list of strengths, or show you areas for improvement. Psychological type does not put us into a box; rather it sorts us according to our innate tendencies and preferences. Once we understand what they are, we can funnel them for more productive uses. Also we can grow or mature within the type (not change type). Moreover, it is clear that no two people are the same within a type as we all have some characteristics of extraversion or introversion, sensing and intuition, thinking and feeling, judging or perceiving. The crucial part is to find out the attitudes and function you prefer. This can ease stress and fatigue.

Extraversion and Introversion: The Attitudes

Carl Jung called introversion and extraversion "attitudes" when discussing how a person receives energy. An "I" person's energy that flows inward prefers the introverted attitude, while those whose energy flows outward prefer the extraverted "E" attitude. Undoubtedly you have seen school children who will jump right into a game or activity while others remain reserved, more reflective. E/I can also be seen at parties—which people are in the middle of the action versus those who stand out on the periphery talking with a few friends. Certainly a given environment will affect whether you approach an event with abandon such as skill level and number of friends. But it is clear that introverts think inwardly and self-reflect while extraverted people talk much more as they think while they are talking. Finally, extraverts gain energy from interaction. An introvert searches for alone time when finished with a prolonged period of being with people. (One caveat here, a middle-age person will often need more solitude). So as you think about what is presented here, try and assess the way you have been for most of your life. You need to focus on the overall pattern of your life. Look at the descriptors that follow and choose the set that best describes your preference. Choose the set that you have felt most comfortable with most of your life. When you have selected your preferred set, circle the word at the top—E or I. Write it here_____.

EXTRAVERSION (E)

When I prefer Extraversion, I am . . .
   Oriented to the outer world
   Focusing on people and things
   Active
   Using trial and error with confidence
   Scanning the environment for stimulation

INTROVERSION (I)

When I prefer Introversion, I am . . .
   Oriented to the inner world
   Focusing on ideas, inner impressions
   Reflective
   Considering deeply before acting
   Finding stimulation inwardly

The next is a perceiving function. One cannot control these; rather it is the way we go about taking in data. Some take it through the five senses, others intuitively through patterns, hunches and reading between the lines. I might ask you to look at a leaf and describe it. Someone who uses the sensing function might say red or thin, while someone relying on the intuitive function may say Leaf (as in Leif Erickson) or a boat for mice. Once again look at the descriptors under the sets that follow and choose a set that best describes your preference. Go with the one you have felt most comfortable with for most of your life. Circle the word at the top. (Intuition is marked by an N so that it won't be confused with introversion.) Write the letter here____.
   Try to ascertain yours now:

SENSING PERCEPTION (S)

When using my Sensing, I am . . .
   Perceiving with the five senses
   Attending to practical and factual details

In touch with the physical realities
Attending to the present moment
Confining attention to what is said and done
Seeing "little things" in everyday life
Attending to step-by-step experience
Letting "the eyes tell the mind"

INTUITIVE PERCEPTION (N)

When using my Intuition, I am . . .
   Perceiving with memory and associations
   Seeing patterns and meanings
   Seeing possibilities
   Projecting possibilities for the future
   Imagining, "reading between the lines"
   Looking for the big picture
   Having hunches, "ideas out of nowhere"
   Letting "the mind tell the eyes"

Thinking and Feeling: The Judging Functions

We use thinking and feeling to evaluate or come to closure about the information we perceived. Thinking and feeling types generally like to come to closure in different ways. Their decision-making process is usually based on either objectivity (thinking) or subjectivity (feeling). Let's just say that you are a manager of a Little League baseball team that's going to the state championships. You're allowed to bring only thirteen players, and you have sixteen on the roster. How do you make the decision on who to bring? What criteria do you use to choose the players who will go? RBIs? Fielding abilities? The fact they were there at every practice? Parental pressure? Loyalty to the team? Think about this scenario and look at the descriptors under the sets that follow and choose the set that best describes your preferences. Again, choose the set that you have felt more comfortable with most of your life. When you have selected your preferred set, circle the word at the top. Place the letter here____.

THINKING JUDGMENT (T)

When reasoning with Thinking, I am . . .
   Using logical analysis
   Using objective and impersonal criteria
   Drawing cause and effect relationships
   Being firm-minded
   Prizing logical order
   Being skeptical

FEELING JUDGMENT (F)

When reasoning with Feeling, I am . . .
  Applying personal priorities
  Weighing human values and motives,
  my own and others
  Appreciating
  Valuing warmth in relationships
  Prizing harmony trusting

Judging and Perceiving: The Orientation to the Outer World

Judging does not mean judgmental; it means when dealing with the outside world one likes to bring things to closure. Those who are usually oriented toward a judging type live in a structured and ordered lifestyle and plan ahead. Those with perceiving type prefer a more flexible lifestyle than judging types and like to keep their options open. For instance, imagine being given $5,000 to spend on a vacation to Disneyland. Those relying on their judging function would make all kinds of detailed plans of how and when—even the best time to take certain rides. Those relying on the perceiving function would "wing" it or stay in the moment. Look over the descriptors in each set of words or phrases and see what appeals to you. If you're in a job that requires a lot of structure, be sure to consider whether or not you feel comfortable with that structure. Examine your real needs when you're considering which set to choose, and then circle the word at the top. Put the letter here_____.

JUDGING (J)

When I take a Judging attitude, I am . . .
  Using thinking or feeling judgment outwardly
  Deciding and planning
  Organizing and scheduling
  Controlling and regulating
  Goal oriented
  Wanting closure, even when data are
  incomplete

PERCEIVING (P)

When I take a Perceiving attitude, I am . . .
  Using sensing or intuitive perception outwardly
  Taking in information
  Adapting and changing
  Curious and interested
  Open-minded
  Resisting closure to obtain more data

Now choose your letters (E or I, S or N, T or F, J or P) and fill them in here_____. Your selection should look something like INTJ, ESFP, ENTP. For more information on the four-digit codes see appendix A, which includes a bit more on the topic, and a bibliography on Jung's cognitive functions.

Our concern in this book has to do with how stress affects each of the sixteen type codes in a burnout situation. For example, let us examine a thirty-four-year-old high school history teacher named Andy who complained of chronic stress and had a strong desire to give up teaching because of the various events he faced daily. He is considering his own writing business helping people get their memories down on paper and is on the verge of quitting his job. Once he takes an MBTI and we examine his Temperaments, Cognitive Codes and Interaction Styles (all of which can be discerned from the Type Indicator), we begin to hone in on his Inferior Function.

The Inferior Function is the *dark aspect* of your personality, the part of yourself that you do not understand very well, the part of your personality that you are prone to avoiding or rejecting. Due to long-term reliance on the dominant function and always choosing its goals and desires, the goals and desires of the inferior function remain submerged in the unconscious mind. However, according to psychoanalytic theory, mental activities that are too repressed in the unconscious mind have a way of exerting themselves underhandedly when you least expect it, which implies that the inferior function is not truly "inferior" but actually quite powerful in ways that you do not fully grasp.

Inferior Function for Each Type:

- ISTJ/ISFJ: Si dominant -> inferior Ne
- INTJ/INFJ: Ni dominant -> inferior Se
- ESTP/ESFP: Se dominant -> inferior Ni
- ENTP/ENFP: Ne dominant -> inferior Si
- ISTP/INTP: Ti dominant -> inferior Fe
- ISFP/INFP: Fi dominant -> inferior Te
- ESTJ/ENTJ: Te dominant -> inferior Fi
- ESFJ/ENFJ: Fe dominant -> inferior Ti

As we grow up, we unconsciously reject the inferior function in order to give the dominant function more energy and control over life. This leads to the inferior function being quite underdeveloped, so you will never be able to use it as well or as comfortably as a dominant function, and this can produce unconscious insecurities. The more heavily you rely on the dominant function, the more you press down on the inferior function, causing it to feel too constricted and bottling up its energy. When you are under intense emotional stress or no longer have the mental energy to maintain the cognitive control of the dominant function, that bottled-up inferior energy has the potential to leak back into the conscious mind, causing a regression to more primitive coping behaviors (this is described by Naomi Quenk as "being **in the grip** of the inferior function") (emphasis added). This makes you act seemingly out of character.

Once the grip period is over, you may wonder why you behaved so badly or what came over you. It is often during these critical times that the inferior function is more visible and memorable because it accompanies negative emotions or the low points in life. Since the inferior function tends to flare up when you lose self-control, it is more likely to manifest in immature, childish, dysfunctional, or destructive behavior. People who are prone to manifesting inferior grip tendencies generally have low self-awareness, are unhappy without understanding why, and their cognitive processes are operating at an instinctual or primal level, driven by unconscious emotional reactivity. If you experience chronic/prolonged periods of "being in the grip," the grip behaviors can obscure or bury your true self, which may lead to mistyping because, at that point, the inferior function has turned your entire personality upside down, making it very difficult to know who you really are.

Let us once again visit the INTP high school teacher. His Inferior or least-used function is Extraverted Feeling.

INTP

Moderate Stress Reaction

- Withdrawal and quietness; increased irritability
- Excessive thinking and cogitating with emphasis on logic; paralysis of analysis
- Intellectually combative and increasingly insensitive to emotional climate

More Extreme Stress Reaction

- Emotional outbursts
- Feelings of not being liked or appreciated
- Forgetfulness, disorganization, confusion

We start the discussion: Do you get forgetful or too easily distracted? Do you feel unfocused, inefficient, and scattered, like you've lost control of yourself, and perhaps even overcompensate by becoming obsessive about proving something to yourself or others? Do you feel like you cannot think straight, as though your mind is a mess (loss of healthy dominant Ti functioning, see appendix A) Do you feel mentally clouded or overwhelmed by negative emotions like confusion, anger, sadness, or frustration? Do you find yourself snapping, whining, or complaining about things that would not normally bug you and perhaps cannot pinpoint the reason why you are behaving that way? Do you feel too entangled by outside influences, especially from the demands, needs, or opinions of other people? Do you become hypersensitive about other people's opinions of you, for example, feeling unlovable, ashamed, or alienated from others? Do you feel an urge to get some kind of affirmation, attention, approval, agreement, or validation from others, trying to impress or provoke or influence people (because you don't know how to connect on a more intimate level)? Do you find yourself becoming irrationally desperate, possessive, or clingy in your relationships? (Inferior Fe acts out insecurely or desperately in relation to other people because of losing self-assuredness when the boundary between self and other becomes increasingly blurred.)

For an INTP, some solutions are like gold.

- Find an entirely new model or idea that gives you perspective on your behavior; find quiet time and space for yourself.
- Remember that real life doesn't always make sense and that people (including you) are intellectual and emotional beings.

Once the INTP teacher has scheduled a weekly quiet time in nature and a daily fifteen-minute walk in a park nearby his home, we begin to focus on the story he tells himself about his life. Particularly where it fits into the Hero's Journey as described by Joseph Campbell and, if a woman, we would look at Maureen Murdock's research on the heroine's journey. The easiest way to get to the heart of the story is by having Andy take Carol S. Pearson's archetypal instrument, which suggests which archetypes are active in his life at present. We'll look at this in the next chapter.

Chapter Five

Of Archetypes and Journeys: Case Studies

From our perspective, each of the twelve archetypes is a story in and of itself. They could also play a part of a longer story as the Scarecrow (Sage), Tin Man (Lover), and Lion (Warrior) were for Dorothy (Seeker).

Let's briefly examine the twelve archetypes that we use. It is notable that some of these are not "traditional" heroes in the sense of having archetypal strength of body or mind. Here are a few interpretations on each of Pearson's archetypes.

INNOCENT

The Innocent, fearing abandonment, seeks safety.

Their greatest strength is the trust and optimism that endears them to others and so gain help and support on their quest.

Their main danger is that they may be blind to their obvious weaknesses or perhaps deny them. They can also become dependent on others to fulfil their heroic tasks.

ORPHAN

The Orphan, fearing exploitation, seeks to regain the comfort of the womb and neonatal safety in the arms of loving parents. To fulfill their quest they must go through the agonies of the developmental stages they have missed.

Their strength is the interdependence and pragmatic realism that they had to learn at an early age. A hazard is that they will fall into the victim mentality and so never achieve a heroic position.

WARRIOR

Warriors are relatively simple in their thought patterns, seeking simply to win whatever confronts them, including the dragons that live inside the mind and their underlying fear of weakness.

Their challenge is to bring meaning to what they do, perhaps choosing their battles wisely, which they do using courage and the warrior's discipline.

CAREGIVER

Caregivers first seek to help others, which they do with compassion and generosity. A risk they take is that in their pursuit to help others they may end up being harmed themselves.

They dislike selfishness, especially in themselves, and fear what it might make them.

SEEKER

Seekers are looking for something that will improve their life in some way, but in doing so may not realize that they have much already inside themselves.

They embrace learning and are ambitious in their quest and often avoid the encumbrance of support from others. Needing to "do it themselves," they keep moving until they find their goal (and usually their true self too).

LOVER

The Lover seeks the bliss of true love and the syzygy of the divine couple.

They often show the passion that they seek in a relationship in their energy and commitment to gaining the reciprocal love of another.

They fear both being alone and losing the love that they have gained, driving them to constantly sustain their love relationships.

DESTROYER

The Destroyer is a paradoxical character whose destructiveness reflects the death drive and an inner fear of annihilation. As a fighter, they are thus careless of their own safety and may put others in danger too.

Their quest is to change, to let go of their anger or whatever force drives them and return to balance, finding the life drive that will sustain them. Living on the cusp of life and death, they are often surprisingly humble.

CREATOR

Creators, fearing that all is an illusion, seek to prove reality outside of their minds.

A critical part of their quest is in finding and accepting themselves, discovering their true identity in relation to the external world.

RULER

The Ruler's quest is to create order and structure and hence an effective society in which the subjects of the Ruler can live productive and relatively happy lives.

This is not necessarily an easy task, as order and chaos are not far apart, and the Rulers have to commit themselves fully to the task. The buck stops with them, and they thus must be wholly responsible—for which they need ultimate authority.

MAGICIAN

The Magician's quest is not to "do magic" but to transform or change something or someone in some way.

The Magician has significant power and as such may be feared. They may also fear themselves and their potential to do harm.

Perhaps their ultimate goal is to transform themselves, achieving a higher plane of existence.

SAGE

The Sage is a seeker after truth and enlightenment and journeys far in search of the next golden nugget of knowledge.

The danger for the sages and their deep fear is that their hard-won wisdom is built on the sand of falsehood. Their best hope is that they play from a position of objective honesty and learn to see with clarity and know truth from and untruth.

JESTER

The goal of the Jester is perhaps the wisest goal of all, which is just to enjoy life as it is, with all its paradoxes and dilemmas.

What causes most dread in the Jester is a lack of stimulation and being "not alive." They must seek to "be," perhaps as the Sage, but may not understand this.

Let's look at our high school teacher (INTP) again. He is thirty-four years old, has chronic stress as and often finds himself in the grip of the Inferior Function (Fe), which we discussed in the preceding chapter. After taking the Pearson Marr Archetype Indicator (PMAI), we find that he has high scores in the Seeker and in the archetypes of Sage and Magician and Creator. He has a very low score in the Orphan Archetype. The Seeker demonstrates a desire to change or a transitional stage in the archetypal Hero's journey. The Magician and Sage demonstrate he has the talent to make the change, and the Creator shows that he has the wherewithal and desire to leap out to do something else.

But do what? If he had a high Destroyer Archetype, we would be concerned about a compulsive jump into something else to throw out a job, a marriage, buy a red sports car, and so on that people often do. But Andy sincerely enjoys his wife and family, and knows that teaching has been his calling since his early years. So, after some discussion with us and a review of his teaching credentials and the Strong Interest Indicator, he decided to involve his principal in the discussion. The result was an opportunity for Andy to create a new AP course in quantitative history that the students loved and Andy found stimulating to teach. He continued to love teaching by finding ways to allow his active archetypes to emerge and flourish. He also found through therapies like Gestalt, talk, narrative, and sand-tray that he became capable to articulate what was bothering him and to stay in his vocation.

A year later, Andy retook the Pearson Instrument and found himself high in the areas of Creator, Magician, Sage, and Jester. By becoming more aware of what was journeying up through the unconscious via the archetypes, he began to see his life as heroic, not pathologic. Life was much better as he became a significant contributor to his school and neighborhood.

Sandra was forty-seven, recently divorced, with two children as seniors in high school, and held a master's in education. She taught at an elementary school for close to twenty years. Visiting with her it soon became apparent that she felt life had not been fair. "I followed the rules and did the things I was told and now face an empty house," she told me. An ENFP, she was tired all the time and saw the future as bleak with only limited opportunities. Teaching fifth grade for the previous eight years had its moments, but as we talked. I felt moved to ask her about staying in education but rather expand herself into another area: career counseling.

ENFPs make great career/life coaches as they often can intuit things about others that those cannot discern about themselves. Give an ENFP time and space, and she has a great capacity to help others articulate their strengths and purposes. She just has to stay away from taking on too much. The PMAI demonstrated that she was high in Ruler, Creator, and Magician and extremely low in Innocent. We began to discuss how the journey of a teacher may take her into new aspects of teaching such as becoming a principal or school counselor. She signed up with a local college that offered counseling classes. Soon she came in brimming with enjoyment as there were at least four women in the class who were making a journey such as hers. She still has a year to go in the course (and remains teaching fifth grade), and her principal cannot promise a position to her as a counselor, but would give Sandra a stellar recommendation. Above all, her principal does promise Sandra something the Innocent score underlines. Sandra will not be abandoned. Sandra is on her way to a life of new opportunities in the teaching vocation.

Dan was fifty-six and taught in a middle school for most of his thirty years of teaching. An ESTJ and principal of a middle school for the past twelve years, he is tired of it all. His PMAI scores indicate burnout: high scores in the Innocent, Orphan, and Ruler and low scores in Creator and Seeker. He hated his life in education, felt betrayed and abandoned by his teachers and current school board, and wanted to quit. Teachers were constantly complaining about low salaries, long hours, and few supplies. Dan felt helpless in the face of the superintendent's desire for all schools to hold their expenses down. The superintendent (an ENTJ) had problems of her own implementing standardized curriculum across the district and dealing with the state board of education.

Ultimately, Dan took a leave of absence, developed some distance from the problems at school, and reenergized his Creator Archetype through the building of homes for the homeless. Upon his return to school, he resigned his job as principal and took a part-time teacher job. When a foreman job opened for Habitat for Humanity, he applied and was hired. Between building homes and building children's lives, he found satisfaction. Upon taking the PMAI a year later, he scored high in Creator, Caretaker, and Ruler. Moreover, he did not feel taken for granted and betrayed. He was on a meaningful journey.

WHAT IS YOUR CASE STUDY?

It is best to find someone you trust to help you articulate what is happening to you in your life right now. Perhaps a good friend who is a fellow teacher. You should find your story—take the MBTI (or a similar instrument) and the PMAI, which to a trained eye, can help you present your current place on the individuation spectrum. You might ask yourself some additional questions like those that follow (see those "Jonah asked" in the chapter 4) that look at the trigger points for "burnout":

• Do I suffer from fatigue—is it chronic?
• Do I suffer from illness?
• Do I suffer from physical or psychological stress?
• Do I suffer from alcohol or drug (including prescriptions) addictions?
• Am I going through significant life transitions?

The key to navigating burnout is getting back to "*the meaningful journey.*" Just like Dorothy and Toto's bypass off the road to OZ where they fell asleep in the poppy field, or Jonah's taking a boat away from his called path, we must ultimately discover the yellow-brick road of individuation again, or we will simply have visited earth as phantoms in the night. Hopefully, by now you should realize that the answer is not necessarily quitting education, but rather using the education profession to advance your own psychological and physical needs. You have been called as a teacher or administrator. Ask "How do I stay the course and grow?" Your own growth will help others to grow as well.

Once you determine the stressors or triggers in your life, you can work getting out from what has you stagnated. Again, find a friend (perhaps in a weekly meeting) and discuss some of the following questions. They may help kick-start your life:

• By what truths am I living my life?
• Where are my patterns?
• Where do I feel stuck?
• What anxiety is aroused when I contemplate alternatives?
• What specific fears can be unpacked from the much vaguer but paralyzing angst?
• Which of those fears is based on childhood experience, with its limited powers and its limited awareness of a larger world?
• Which of those fears are likely to happen?
• Can you bear them happening?
• What will happen to you if you do not bear them, and you stay stuck?
• Can you risk being a larger person?
• Can you bear the pain of growth over the pain of remaining afraid, small, and lost?
• Can you accept that, at the end of your life, you were not here?
• Can you bear to only have been a phantom, a victim of fate, a refuge from destiny?

- Can you bear having been only a troubled guest on this earth without making some part of it yours?
- Can you face these questions?
- Can you live with yourself not facing these questions, now that you know they exist?
- Can these questions recover your journey for you?
- Can they? Can you?

Study the following poem titled "The Holy Longing" by J. W. von Goethe and answer its clarion call:

> And so long as you haven't experienced
> This: to die and so to grow
> You are only a troubled quest
> On the dark earth.

The point is that when we feel tense, anxious, depressed, vague, or exhausted, we are most likely at a threshold of transformation, of a call to a larger life teeming with energy, intention, and promise. When life seems flat, uninteresting, completely routine, or too narrow, we are circling the field of call. When loss has us feeling robbed, directionless, purged, or even relieved but misplaced, we might be in the maze of a call. When we stumble upon a new idea, a new interest, and a different perspective, we may discover an unplowed field of call. Teaching is a vocation to which you are called. Let the muses guide you on the path of this unknown sea, and you will find authenticity in living an individuated life.

Chapter Six

"The University of the Waves": An Encounter for Archetypal Reflectivity

I need the sea because it teaches me.
I don't know if I learn music or awareness,
if it's a single wave or its vast existence,
or only its harsh voice or its shining
suggestion of fishes and ships.
The fact is that until I fall asleep,
in some magnetic way I move in
the university of the waves.
                    —Pablo Neruda, *On the Blue Shore of Silence*, 2003a, p. 3

AN ENCOUNTER FOR ARCHETYPAL REFLECTIVITY

Many years ago I taught in an international school that was located at the foot of the Andean mountains, on acres of green with palms, parakeets, and geckos. As a faculty of international and Colombian teachers, we worked collaboratively to develop interdisciplinary curricula across the grade ten subject areas. We were intentional about respecting a rhythmic cycle of learning based on A. N. Whitehead's educational theory. Students' curiosities, interests, and passions were central to the paced acquisition of skills and their ensuing application to fecund particularities within their own lives. Their delight in learning was paramount to any grammar and generalization.

Many of the multilingual students were well read and well traveled. And many were fatefully situated in socio-political issues. That is, they were aware of familial, even ancestral, suffering and sacrifices interwoven with the turbulent history of the place they called home.

Despite the tension of the times—Cali, Colombia, during the mid-1990s—there was joy to be found in the love of music, family, and tradition. While the country was pulled apart through internal and external strive via cocaine, cartels, and corruption, school days were similarly interrupted with unrest—preparations for evacuations, contingency plans regarding kidnappings, and military surveillance by loud, low, armed flyovers (helicopters). It was a place where unexpectedly Poetry, Silence, and the Sea became part of a larger language of inquiry.

In many ways, it was this teaching and learning experience that permitted me to explore, embody, even experiment with Poetry—the Poetic—as a way of being-and-becoming, as a doing, not-doing, even undoing, and the beautiful Thing itself. That is, it was a place and time that allowed me to turn to the imaginal and poetic basis of consciousness. Such exploration unfolded both within my English language arts classes and beyond the school's secured perimeter to outreach projects in literacy and ecology with students in neighboring communities.

This opportunity presented itself after my fifth year of secondary school teaching, a pivotal time, when many teachers become disheartened or overwhelmed and quit the profession. I sought international teaching as a way to sidestep the politics of a small town, as I was the only female teacher in the high school, and the administrative demands on public education teachers, although minimal compared to today's realities. I just wanted to be teaching and learning with the students and the issues central to the discipline. This opportunity was also on the heels of completing a masters' degree that was founded on the desire to teach for purposeful encounters conjoining students, the subject matter, and the realities confronting our world, both local and global.

This crucial time, when teachers question themselves and the profession, could be bolstered by a regenerative reflective practice with meaningful symbols and a richer understanding of life's inherent patterns. Such practice could aid teachers to resacralize their work. Teachers who feel called to teaching, yet worn out or dried up by the un/expected and un/accounted for, can experience rejuvenation by recognizing they play parts in narratives that exceed the local and individual—narratives that parallel those of heroes, royals, magicians, and lovers, even sages, shamans, artists, and activists (Campbell, 1949; Fidyk, 2010; Lindley, 1993; Mayes, 2010; Moore & Gillette, 1990; Wolff, 1951; Wyatt, 2017).

These narratives unfold through three aspects of the universe—matter, meaning, and energy—whereby each aspect enfolds the other two in an ongoing process of creative becoming. For Whitehead, this is the "principle of universal relativity," the mutual participation of "being present in another entity" (1941, p. 50) Such process reflects an animated universe, a *mundus imaginalis*, as coined by Ibn Arabi, an Islamic mystic. This realm includes the psychoid, central fire, the unified field, and the collective unconscious, with its realms of spirits, ancestors (primate, animal, archetypal), and subtle (imaginal) bodies. Becoming through a deep connection to *mundus imaginalis* requires a union, a *coniunctio*, between body and spirit, which might lead to awareness of the dynamic energetic fields—somatic and morphic—between-two, which can further facilitate individual and collective individuation, healing, and transformation.

Just as "myth tells how through the deeds of supernatural beings, a reality came into existence" (Fidyk, 2010, p. 2), older narratives "touch and exhilarate centers of life beyond the reach of vocabularies of reason and coercion" (Campbell, 1949, p. 4). From this view, I was in need of exhilaration—an elixir, a *caelum*, a "blue liquid."[1] That "heavenly substance hidden in the body," that evolves from a process of reconnecting emotions and feeling with consciousness, and the eventual union of spirit with body, that is lured out by the "art" of inner work (Jung, *CW* 14, par. 681). I had arrived at a place where there was an unsaid yet deeply felt obligation to teach and live from my own authenticity, while encouraging the same from other(s) with whom I was in relation.

Teaching was no longer about content, methods, and "curriculum-as-planned" as it often is during the initial years (Aoki, 1986/1991/2005). And it was no longer for evaluation of teacher performance—the condition to achieve a permanent contract. I could no longer give a grades to students whose test performance did not reflect their[2] knowing. Subject matter had to come alive through students' interests and engagement, which affected the pace, design, and meaning of learning. Teaching, for me, became a search to learn by way of relatedness—a respect *of* or a reverence *for* what Martin Buber (1958) called *I-Thou* relationships—a living relation with other. That is, the other as subject, not separate or separated by discrete bounds, and where the "I" does not objectify, be it tree, air, or child (i.e., *I-It*). The "It" of *I-It* refers to the world of experience and sensation—physical only.

TEACHING AND LEARNING BY WAY OF RELATEDNESS

Before beginning the amplification of the symbols central to this teaching encounter, I explore the "way of relatedness" as a pedagogical and ethical orientation to teaching and learning. The way of relatedness kept me in relation, not only with myself, but also with students, place, words, the unknown, and the not-yet lived.

In I-Thou relationships, a Buberian "I" reaches toward a You. In its relation with the Thou, Buber's I is further related to itself by means of the Thou. That is, the I is "related to the Thou as to someone who in turn relates itself to the I, as though it came into delicate contact with himself through the skin of the Thou" where all the while, the I preserves its active reality (Levinas in Schilpp, Friedman, & Buber, 1967, p. 142). For Buber, this is the "realm of the interhuman"—"the sphere of the ethical and our only access to the divine" (Orange, 2010, p. 91).

I-Thou describes the world of relations—as living entities in a dynamic web of interrelations rather than separate and hierarchical, one-directional lines/lives—that continuously touch one another. "Touch is what first *affects* us, and does so in the most concrete, singular ways. . . . To touch and be touched simultaneously is to be *connected* with others in a way that enfolds us" (Kearney, 2015, p. 21). In my reading of the *I-Thou* relationship, the hyphen means: touch, contact, connection. It is a carnal and energetic bond between-two that symbolizes sacred resonance, yet it is not of them only. Whether the hyphen is called the third, liminal or borderland space, its existence points to the transformative energy that rises between-two while simultaneously held and patterned by the creative pulse of existence. In this connection, a third emerges—something of each, something of their two-getherness, and something not-yet-known. When we engage students wherein we lose our edges, we emulate the wisdom of the universe and partake in a co-creative process on a microcosmic level.

This "between" can be understood as flesh—a shared membrane between body and world—"a specific bond of belonging" (Gadamer cited in Orange, 2010, p. 1). In the ancient wisdom of Aristotle,

> flesh is both what makes the world appear (as touching-speaking) and what belongs to the world (as touch-spoken). . . . A twofold ontological texture— feeling and felt—which provides the underlying unity between the becoming-body of my senses and the becoming-world of my body. (Kearney, 2015, p. 38)

As such, the hyphen as flesh can be read as the sincere gesture, "delicate contact," that calls us to responsibility and hospitality *and* disrupts the myriad ways in which we reduce and objectify each other. It resists collapse into the binaries of matter and form, soul and substance, but it is to be understood as an "ontological element" in which we already find ourselves (p. 38). Touch, which extends the carnal, and freshly concretizes relations, includes the nonhuman worlds of animal and plant. With this inclusion Buber's notion of "interhuman" is best revised to "inter-post-human" or switched for Thich Nhat Hanh's "interbeing" so to erase humans at the center and put us back into lateral relations with animals, trees, and technology.

The vibrational energy between-two bodies is experienced somatically— a felt sense or a somatic resonance (Latin *resonantia*, "echo," from *resonare*, "resound")—a term that originates from the field of acoustics. It includes experiences such as empathy, mirroring, intuition, attunement, and kines-thetic sensing. Somatic resonance is a mutual process, involving both par-ties. It is also the awareness of what is taking place in the somatic field—that is, what is palpable and perceptible between my porous flesh and the flesh of a student, the sun, or the sea. In this way, the interiority of my flesh condi-tions the exteriority of the world, rather than opposing it. The more my flesh feels, and thus feels itself, the more the world is opened. And when flesh exposes itself immediately to another flesh, without translation, without a thing, without anything as intermediary, it bares itself. Strikingly, "I feel the world depending on whether I feel myself!" (Marion, 2007, p. 214).

As if nested rings, resonant, vibrational bodies exist within a second field. This second field, a morphic field, imposes patterns on random or rather indeterminate patterns of activity. Morphic fields are not fixed but evolve through a kind of nonlocal resonance. They are acquired as a kind of biological inheritance where each individual has access to a collective memory from the past members of its species and also contributes to the collective memory, affecting future members of the species (Sheldrake, 1995/2012). While we circle back to these fields later, the point here is that there are many more elements affecting relations than the visible and known.

Somatic resonance, best described as mother-child attunement, is often likened to what is experienced in "good" psychotherapeutic relationships. It is also central to creative and pedagogic ones because it is encountered as carnal contact with self, other, and something beyond both—be it the creative potential of the cosmos, the divine, or the ancestors. Somatic awareness of self, itself a felt fleshy body, is our most fundamental experience because through it we access our interiority.

When we attune to others in an empathetic and non-judgmental way, it "enables them to develop an awareness of their inner states and to experience, contain, and express the full range of emotions" (Stromsted, 2015, p. 57). We are also able to witness the messages of our inner voice(s) and experience a deep internal feeling of stability, consistency, the wonder of being alive, and a nonverbal body sensation of truth and authenticity. When our sense of self is not grounded in our bodies, not only do we miss the experience but also we lack a sense of calm or ease that comes from trust that rests at this center. To avoid the feeling of dis-ease, some look outside themselves for that which is crucial to being and/or substitute "doing" behaviors.

Without body awareness, many fall into this substitute category where each thing is experienced as separate (*I-It*). "It" stands in contrast to "Thou": *It* relations (I-*It*) are understood as "I have many separate and distinct relations with each 'It' (student)"—dependent upon the Its within one's life. Living relatedness experienced through care and a felt energetic connection (as symbolized by *I-Thou*) fosters students' well-being. That is, this kind of contact or touch enhances socio-emotional, psycho-spiritual, and physical health intellectual curiosity and growth; as well as ethical development through ecological and aesthetic appreciation.

Archetypal reflectivity, a mode of teacher reflection moves beyond the common, singular forms of cultural, political, or autobiographical reflection. It delves more deeply into the complexity of teachers' ontological constructs and commitments, which are inter- and multicultural/spiritual/political—even somatic. Such reflectivity bridges these factors with the particularities of the teacher's inner world, together held and influenced by life's creative enfolding. When engaging in archetypal reflectivity, teachers are better able to draw upon the "*mana*—the psychospiritual life blood of teaching"—to experience greater joy and efficacy in their work, while simultaneously knowing that they are connected to more than current place and time (Mayes, 2010, p. 69). Such touch was what I sought in both my teaching and my life.

THE ARCHETYPAL PULL OF POETRY, SILENCE, AND THE SEA

My own teaching, writing, and research over the past 25 years have been enlivened through conscious relationship with the collective unconscious and the unified field. In particular, the archetypal influence of Poetry, Silence, and the Sea have been transformative.[3] In what follows, examples of each are interwoven as a textual pastiche—memories and reflections of that Colombian experience, interwoven with photographs, philosophical musings, and pedagogical potentialities. These elements intertwined with archetypal amplification—a process of enlargement by way of thought pattern, feeling, and emotional experience through a multitude of parallels. Together, they seek to evoke the very Things championed rather than an exposition about them.

Just as Silence "uses [a] system to draw what needs saying further along" (Lilburn, 2002, p. 2), this writing, in contact with the very things it seeks to illustrate, does the organizing, the laying bare, the bringing to consciousness. Despite the "I" or "author" who contributes her pressing to know, she must yield to where the writing wants to go. Many philosophers and poets of this tradition say that "what is wanted is a kind of negative attention, an alert emptiness"[4] (p. 2). In following this lineage, this text then is not an unravelling of a single thought or argument, nor a guide on how to proceed. There is no position or technique where language comes to claim and bring closure—just the drift of attunement to three archetypal images. Here, "the writing has an open ear, [and] proceeds by this ear" (p. 2).

Let us turn to the time when against adverse circumstances of murder, drug smuggling, hijacking, and bombing, sixty grade ten students and seven teachers flew to the Colombian coast where we sailed by fishing vessel to Gorgona— Parque Nacional Natural Gorgona—an island, a nature preserve, in the Pacific Ocean. Here lessons unfolded amid grueling hikes, night swims, and the dance of shadow and light. These events transformed not only our relationships and so learning, but also our selves—even if suspended in space and time like seeds laid dormant. I did not know then what years hence would bear—the ways in which those seeds would root and proliferate in my professional and personal unfolding.

Looking back, those years in Colombia might best be described as stepping into the Poetic as an orientation to Living. Doing so asked, what might this endeavor mean to our personal and communal responsibilities within current educational contexts? And in what ways might it affect our actions? Responding in part through the spirit of Pablo Neruda (recognizably Chilean, not Colombian), his life and poetry, this work reflects the dynamism that unfolds through the creative impulses experienced in relation with an archetypal

source: art, more precisely, Poetry. In this account, poetry appears as an ethical, spiritual, political, even somatic act where it came from afar, morphed
through years and across continents, only to be taken up again in a northern
parkland during a midcareer collapse. What might it mean for teaching and
learning, for curriculum and pedagogy, to call upon Poetry as guide?

In the very least, poetry synthesizes experience in a direct and affective
way; it amplifies and enlivens; it distills; it bears witness; and, it binds us
to life while opening us up to more than the possible. And yet, it honors the
past—phantoms and ancestors—those who have come before us, be they
bloodlines, ink-lines, or song-lines—understood as Indigenous memory, code,
or transgenerational memory. Poetry points ahead to what may never be; and
yet, it encourages us to imagine it, to fight for it. Its process is performative
for it derived from an oral art form deeply rooted in a sense of voice and
community. Yet, it contains experiences belonging to the deepest and darkest
of events.

C. G. Jung wrote similarly of "life-lines constructed by the hermeneutic
method" always temporary "for life does not follow straight lines whose
course can be predicted in advance," and "never general principles or univer-
sally accepted ideas but points of view and attitudes that have a provisional
life" (cited in Stein, 2006a, p. 145). In the revisitation of this particular
teaching event, "it is not a matter of applying universals to cases but instead
of applying cases, [or a case, as this case may be,] to universals" (Caputo in

Moules, McCaffrey, Field, & Laing, 2015, p. x). That might sound strange because of the inverted nature of "case"—which comes from *cadere, casum*, to fall—as in casualty. The implied meaning is that:

> the individual represents a "fall" from the truth and reality of the universal, a decline into mere particularity. But this is to invert reality for the individual is what is real . . . the first truth, the true being, while universals are abstractions . . .—siphoned off (abstract = *ab* + *trahere*) individuals. (p. x)

As such, hermeneutics, a method that shares kinship with the lyrical (from Hermes's invention of the lyre), is better served to speak not of the individual case but of the singular situation, "not of 'cases' but of 'singularities,' which are always marked by a certain alterity, idiomaticity, idiosyncrasy, and conceptual impenetrability" (Caputo in Moules et al., 2015, p. x). Singularities are not a fall, deficiency, casualty, or lack; rather, they are "an excess, far too rich to ever be adequately explicated into generalities" (p. x). The wisdom of hermeneutics alerts us "to the delicate art of practice" and to the "practical wisdom" demanded of the educator, whereby "the method is not a method except in its etymological sense of *meta*—making one's way along the path (*odos*) to truth" (p. xi).

Engaging in archetypal reflectivity like hermeneutics and the poetic reveals those on both sides of the image, the rhythm, the form, as both "masked and unmasked, costumed and bared, liars and truth-tellers, actors and audience, offstage and onstage" (Prendergast, 2009, p. xxiii). When other forms of language fail, the work of poets across time, who have written about social injustice, poverty, war, alienation, and so on, offers inspiration, compassion, even *ways through*, and reminds us of the potential of poetry, regardless of the events. As Kearney (2015) writes of carnal hermeneutics, "Matter, no less than form, is about what matters—to us, to others and to the world in which we breathe and have our being. The old dichotomies between 'empirical' and 'transcendental,' 'materialism' and 'idealism,' are ultimately ruinous" (p. 15).

As such, if a poet's investiture is to remember whence we came, to ask who we are as individuals and simultaneously who we are as communities, and to wonder where we are headed, what might this mean pedagogically? Ontologically? After all, the poetic, creative, and imaginal lie at the heart of a symbolic approach to education—that which is increasingly vital not only as an antidote to the destructive emphasis on technical rational education with its reliance upon materialism, measurability, and abstraction but also as a balm to psychological wounds and trauma through right-brain-to-right-brain affective embodied experiences. Without a dynamic counterpoint to this polarity, education falls dangerously into an extreme where its implications impact every aspect of life, most immediately the affective and somatic modes where imagination and the spiritual reside.

POETIC GESTURE, SINGULARITY, AND METHOD

To more fully understand this poetic gesture, let us lean into translator William O'Daly's description of Pablo Neruda's singularity, his method:

> [W]hen Neruda composed his poems, he gave himself to the process as if he were still the small boy in his own dream, surrounded at the family feast by gunfire and smoke, guitars and wine. In that dream . . . he is dressed in black and holds a cup of still-warm lamb's blood to his lips—terrified, dying like the lamb and toasting to joy, he drinks the blood. The imagery represented for Neruda a willingness to accept his investiture as a human being and as a poet, whose anguish and joy derive from his response to the world. (in Neruda, 2002a, pp. x–xii).

In what ways do educators reflect upon what was taught, not taught, and untaught as our response to other, to the world? If we assessed this "doing"—as reflective of our responsibility as human beings—would that change "the what," and "the way of teaching"? What would it say of the *"pedagogic being"* that we are, that each of us is (Aoki, 1986/1991/2005, p. 161, emphasis added)?

Analogous to Neruda and poetry, Michel Sciacca, the Italian philosopher and teacher, said: "Philosophy for me has been and is life and not an academic exercise or an intellectual curiosity" (Sciacca cited in Farinella, 1976, p. 144) "It is my need," he writes, "to fertilize spirits, to agitate problems and to feel myself fertilized by the others" (p. 144). This lived practice, an earthy wisdom, carried him to many countries in order to dialogue with diverse people and to share his discoveries in the realm of the spirit. The need "to feel myself fertilized by the others," that is, both revitalized and nourished by dialogue or contact with others was also mine, in teaching then and now. How might educators' responses take on a poetic basis of mind—that is, how might an aim or intention be conceived as poetic, lyric, or mythic rather than bound by literalism, rationalism, and empiricism?

Perhaps it was in response to that world: the Colombian tempo, a riotous mix of Spanish, African, and Native American cultures and histories; the enduring spirit required amid social and political upheaval; or the late nights reading Neruda to a backdrop of salsa and symphony, but I came to realize that "a poet's oeuvre lives not in any single deed or inspired turn of phrase." (O'Daly in Neruda, 2002a, xvii). Rather, it lives in the fact that *it is a chosen life.* A life chosen, fated, as familial inheritance, even before we are small children—paradoxically both terrifying and joyous. It is a response to both conscious and unconscious callings. Such a life is founded upon a fluid "commitment to values and action inspired by the desire for truth and justice, an idea invented by the troubadours in the thirteenth century" (p. xvii).

Despite the complexity of "truth and justice" today, these desires endure. Such a commitment remains radically communal, never separate, never unrelated. These values stitch us with all that has been, continuously opening into the present, while simultaneously signaling the plurality and potentiality of what might be. Yet, they are never bound by linearity or causality. Here bifurcate junctures are fully free. That is, in the moment prior to emergence, the path to be taken has not yet been determined—colonized. In this profound ebb and flow of existence, we realize that Life too unfolds and Things come in search of us. As Neruda (1969) pens:

> it was at that age . . . Poetry arrived
> in search of me. I don't know, I don't know where
> it came from, from winter or a river.
> I don't know how or when,
> no, they were not voices, they were not
> words, nor silence,
> but from a street I was summoned,
> from the branches of night,
> abruptly from the others,
> among violent fires
> or returning alone,
> there I was without a face
> and it touched me. (p. 7)

To detect and discern what beckons demands the ability to be present. In other words, one must have developed the capacity, or maintained the ability to be grounded, and attuned, within a body that notices subtle and bodily sensations—which are more than merely physical. One, too, must learn to maintain that inner calm in response to images, thoughts, intuitions, or sensations; and feel, sense, know how to relate from that place to be with-other. The technical term is *interoception*—Latin for "looking inside." Without the capacity for self-awareness, the subtle, sensual, and sensorial world within—and so without—is largely off limits. Such is the work of the Shaman, Sage, and Poet whose ontological and epistemological orientations,[5] like those of Hermes, reflect an ongoing negotiation between inner and outer worlds—which in actuality are one.

Attentiveness of this sort is *in part* akin to what Maxine Greene (1995) calls *wide-awakeness*. Wide-awakeness—"awareness of what it is to be in the world"—provides a philosophical, not abstracted but thoughtful, intentional, even poetic, orientation to life (p. 35). For Greene, wide-awakeness is fundamental to imagination, possibility, and social change because "without the ability to think about yourself, to reflect on your life, there's really no awareness, no consciousness. Consciousness . . . comes through being alive, awake, curious and often furious" (Teaching wide-awake, 2008). However, while not directly stated by Greene and scholars/educators who use her work, such thinking must be embodied—body, mind, and soul.

That is, the thinker must be present, *in relation* to looking inside *and* outside—into the world—local, global, cosmic. The thinker who is "in his head" is disconnected from his body and so the body of Life—using thinking or intellectualism as a defense mechanism or dissociative response. Thinking that occurs in relation to the thinker's felt body/being (embodied soul) *and* to other as person, animal, or culture is attuned to both. Only when present and attuned is empathy possible.[6] Thinking that is detached from embodied awareness ultimately separates, even conquers, as it cuts off from both self and other. Most in schooling and academe are not familiar with the radically different felt experience of these two kinds of thinking. In fact, schooling, as commonly structured, and teachers, as commonly educated, have taught, reinforced, and rewarded thinking that is cut off from sensations, feelings, emotions, intuitions, images, and the wider energetic world.

Greene (2007), through her call for wide-awakeness, advocates for the arts in education not for teaching students the basics of design but for creating the possibility for "a new dimension of a self-in-the-making" (cited in Teaching wide-awake, 2008). Indeed, neuroscience research and studies on trauma show that the only way "we can change the way we feel is by becoming aware of our inner experience and learning to befriend what is going on inside ourselves" (van der Kolk, 2014, p. 206).

Akin to Greene's wide-awakeness, Paulo Freire (1998) called for "critical consciousness"—*conscientization*—raising consciousness to lay bare oppression and to liberate the capacity to learn, imagine, act, and openly dialogue with others in the world. Freire understands *conscientization* as an unfinished "requirement of the human condition . . . as a road we have to follow to deepen our awareness of the world of facts, of events, of the demands of human consciousness to develop our capacity for epistemological curiosity" (p. 55). For Greene (2005), facts are mere givens; so, it is only through imaginative works that we discover "human presences" (p. 3).

For Adrienne Rich (2001), "Art is our human birthright"; "our most powerful means of access to our own and another's experience and imaginative life" (p. 103). Further, "in continually rediscovering and recovering the humanity of human beings, art is crucial to the democratic vision" (p. 103). Here Rich echoes Jung. Despite the cost of emergence of artworks to the artist, Jung (1921/1990) viewed artists as people indispensable to society, as "indispensable . . . to the psychic life of a people" (para. 658). In his estimation, they possess a prophetic force because they express potentialities of ideas from which new sources of energy and consciousness might emerge. They indicate what the spirit of the culture most needs (Fidyk, 2014).

Central to pedagogy enacting these aims, educators "must be awake, critical, open to the world" (Greene, 2005, p. 80). Especially in times like these—global conflict, species extinction, ecological destruction, and human brutality—Greene tasks us: "It is an honor and a responsibility to be a teacher in such dark times—and to imagine, and to act on what we imagine" (p. 80). Jung agrees. For him, there is a fluidity across educator, artist, and activist: "The artist is a *creator* and *educator*, for [their] works have the value of symbols that adumbrate lines of future development" (1921/1990, para. 720). Simply, here "lies the social significance of art: it is constantly at work educating the spirit of the age, conjuring up the forms in which the age is most lacking" (para. 130). As Whitehead (1929/1957) put it: Beauty "should be for action" (p. 47).

When an educator, philosopher, or artist critically imagines anew and possesses great conviction, convincing expression, and maturity of personhood, he reveals another way. We can understand such individuals as living in conscious relation with the unconscious energy of the archetypal images of Wise One, and in some cases, the Rebel, Subversive, Walkaway[7] (Fidyk, 2013b), and Hero (Mayes, 2010)—remembering that the particular forms of these images are in relation to the singularities of a place and time. Yet they are not bound by them. For example, someone in North America embodying the essence of a Hero—to those within the dominant discourse, they most likely would use the moniker Rebel or Subversive because that person acts against status quo—might do so in a shape not known previously to that culture, such as NFL quarterback, Colin Kaepernick (and other players) "taking a knee" in protest to systemic racism. Here Freire's apt phrase applies: "Whoever teaches learns in the act of teaching, and whoever learns teaches in the act of learning" (1998, p. 31).

The characteristics and values of the Hero, however, will be recognizable: one who is called to leave the "simple pleasures, easy routines, and comfortable security of home, clan, and village in order to go alone into an arena of trials and tribulations" (Mayes, 2010, p. 12). Their expressions, thoughts, images are so fresh and alluring that others becomes "mesmerized by the texts [mediums] as much as by the ideas. This is (the power of) the 'strong poet'" (Rautins & Ibrahim, 2011, p. 25). This mesmerizing or seducing capacity of works of art— not the poet who nevertheless is 'strong'—can evoke a numinous moment—an experience of merging, conjoining viewer/participant, artwork, and spirit, and an ensuing body sense of awe. As numinous, the artworks invite the projections—beautiful, disturbing, great—of their viewers. In this way, the outer world of things, Art, thus provides the medium through which the unconscious can be activated and if that activation is made conscious, it can tend toward increased development. As Freire (2007) described, "It is *dreaming* and *existing* that 'allows' us to keep making ourselves into beings who fight for liberation, *Being More*" (p. xi, emphasis in original).

Fascination or seduction via the numinous was understood by Jung (1930/1978) as a "re-immersion in the state of *participation mystique*"—an experience of oneness by fusion (para. 162). At this level of experience, "the secret of artistic creation and of the effect which great art has upon us . . . is no longer [about] the weal or woe of the individual . . . but the life of the collective" (para. 162). That is, the creation that fuels a numinous experience in the participant is not due to the personality of the artist. In fact, it is not even the "I," author, or poet "creating"; rather, the artist is the conduit or vessel through which the creative energy (of an archetype or spirit) moves. The creative urge channels through the poet, embodied momentarily although not affected by her strengths, limitations, or autobiographical details. For the artwork itself already has been imprinted with a pattern by the Life pulse from which it emerged thereby directing its potential be(com)ing. The artwork—poetry—is a response of this planetary life toward the "singularities" of a specific culture and time, serving both as a commentary *upon* them and a salve *for* them.

A great artist, or in this case, the "Strong Poet," according to Richard Rorty (1989), does not simply write verses. Instead, he or she has both the language and the vision to offer us something new or to "invent the known in an unknown language" (p. 25). That is, the strong poet writes deeply meaningful or politically poignant poems as a conduit for the creative pulse of the universe—unlike the lesser artist who might well create through his personality or subjectivity ("I"-ego). The Strong Poet, Rorty explains, is horrified at being "a copy or a replica"; he or she has the courage and audacity to engage, to look for, and address the "blind impresses all our behavings bear," the gaps, the impasses (p. 34), —"the difficult knowledge" that many prefer not to see (Pitt & Britzman, 2003, p. 755). Gaps and impasses, as existent in education that has become reshaped by business models and corporate interests, arise when the leading culture develops itself unilaterally.

These are the cracks where strong poets and great works of art break forth as the collective unconscious of an organization, infrastructure, culture, or country seeks greater stability. As Jung explains:

> Whenever conscious life becomes one-sided or adopts a false attitude, these images "instinctively" rise to the surface in dreams and in the visions of artists and seers to restore the psychic balance, whether of the individual or of the epoch. (Jung, 1930/1978, para. 160)

Neruda (1977), referring to his own era, writes:

> It has been the privilege of our time—with its wars, revolutions, and tremendous social upheavals—to cultivate more ground for poetry than anyone had ever imagined. The common man has had to confront it, attacking or attacked, in solitude or with an enormous mass of people at public rallies. (p. 253)

Poetry or the Poetic calls not only as epistemology—knowing, not-knowing and unknowing—but also as ontology—being-and-becoming through a rhythimic perpetual pulse of creativity. That is, it offers a psychical image of the Strong Poet whose psychospiritual and ontological orientation sits at the core of the human condition (as state of being and action: verb *and* person/thing: noun). As such, it can "serve politically, psychologically, pedagogically, and ethically liberatory purposes—or not" (Mayes, 2017, p. 16).

While the metaphor of the Strong Poet rings deep within current Canadian curriculum studies (Ng-A-Fook, Ibrahim, & Reis, 2016; Rautins & Ibrahim, 2011), it may not be a resonant image for teachers in public education—despite the ripeness of the cultural milieu. But for some of the Colombian students with whom I sat around the fire, there was a sense of "call to adventure" wherein they yearned to address the corruption, oppression, and injustices of their country, while hopeful and desirous of love, courage, compassion, and fairness.

"RESONANT ECOLOGY," *PHRONESIS,* AND SILENCE

Your form extends beyond breakers,
vibrant, and rhythmic, like the chest, cloaking
a single being, and its breathings,
that lift into the content of light,
plains raised above waves,
forming the naked surface of earth.
You fill your true self with your substance.
You overflow curve with silence. (Neruda, n.d.a)

It was as if on those isolated shores, away from the familiar and the expected, the students grew expansive, capable of touching both light and dark sides of themselves and their situations. It was as if on those shores, they stood in a borderland space, capable of imagining *ways through* that were not possible within the confines of Cali. It was as if they knew that "maturation of soul entails that each of us integrate both sides of the archetypes that circulate within us—which is yet another way of understanding the idea of individuation" (Mayes, 2017, pp. 70–71).

As we leaned into the waning night, a premonitory tremor rippled through our conversations. I could hear "the questing soul's frank recognition of and confrontation with its shadow . . . the precondition of emotional, intellectual, and ethic evolution" (Mayes, 2017, p. 71). On this, Neruda (1984) pens:

Perhaps the duties of the poet have been the same throughout history. Poetry was honored to go out into the streets, to take part in combat after combat. When they called him rebel, the poet was not daunted. Poetry is rebellion. The poet is not offended if he is called subversive. Life is more important than societal structures, and there are new regulations for the soul. (p. 349)

Taking heed of "new regulations for the soul," I continue to follow Neruda (1977) as I amplify silence as an archetypal force: "I shall take up those images [of long ago] without attention to chronological order, just like these waves that come and go" (p. 77).

Let us again turn to the island.

I am sitting on the beach. It is as if the sound of the waves I hear now touched something inside me again and again unfolding through the years. Sitting quietly in half lotus, I open my eyes and turn to my left, then right. I count seven students sitting similarly. I hear the low murmur of the waves, water gliding in to caress the shore, sink into the sand, then a slow reluctant move back out to the depths, gathering into itself, then again the sensuous glide forward, reaching out toward the other, a kind of longing and daring in that movement out from oneself.

In equal segments along the beach, we slowly turn with the earth to face the sun. We wait, cross-legged. We attend our breath as it draws forth with the retreating waves and the pull of the moon. Like the breath moving through our bodies, bringing the other inside each of us like water mingling with sand, two different elements mixing, borrowing, giving life to each other. We send the spent breath out, back into the ocean of air all around to be recharged, just as the sea withdraws to its own depths before again gliding forward to caress and sink into the sand. Here—"being in the interconnectedness, the

resonant ecology, of things"—we learned to let go, to give ourselves to the movement of something greater than ourselves, knowing we were related (Zwicky, 2003, p. 86).

"To be wise," writes poet and philosopher Jan Zwicky (2003), "is to grasp another form of life without abandoning one's own; to be able to translate experience in and out of two original tongues" (p. 94). "One can no more hope to understand metaphor if one is not sure the 'real world' exists, than one can hope to understand music if one does not have a body" (Zwicky, 2003, p. 43). Receptive, subtle, patient—perhaps only fleetingly—we glimpsed the whole within the parts. We resisted "the translation that is a form of reduction"— trusting each fragment of life to reveal the depth of existence (p. 94). Outside the classroom, on those far-away shores, our learning emphasized a curiosity, openness, and uncertainty toward interpretation and the relational emphasis on engaged understanding. We fell into a kind of practical wisdom, *phronesis*— discovering first hand the right thing to do in a given situation. Right action or right thought was, in other words, relational accountability as an ethic emerges through bodies in touch with one another and rooted in place.

Just as hermeneutics is the art of interpretation, the art of judgment, and "judgment is the art of the concrete, [t]he person of judgment, Aristotle's *phronimos*, has cultivated the art of discernment" (Caputo cited in Moules et al., 2015, p. xiii). That is, the art of "seeing into the singularity of the situation, into the unexpected demands of the singular, seeing what the situation is calling for, hearing what calls to us in this situation" (p. xiii). Here we find ourselves called—and thus, we respond to what calls upon us. This we do in the only responsible way. As such, hermeneutics is the "maximization of responsibility" as opposed to the flight from responsibility as frequently heard today: "I followed the rules. But I don't make the rules" (p. xiii). Rules reflect abstracted systems of ethics that require little relatedness to the singularities of the case. In fact, most systems have lost their original ethos of care. As Strong Poets, Walkaways, and Heroes know, rules are not always the right thing to follow.

> The universality of hermeneutics means that such discernment is called for in every branch of life—not only in ethics, but in art . . . and in science. . . . Hermeneutics is not a theory of knowledge but the art of life and death, and . . . Hermeneutics takes the risk of embracing the coming of what we cannot see coming. (p. xiii)

Quieting the mind, tracking the breath, incorporating ritual, including the arts and creative processes, and attending the body through embodied through embodied presence, while aspects of contemplative practice, serve as a foundation to live ethically, to live poetically, especially when they involve interaction between conscious and unconscious states. Such practice solicits images of the Elder, Wise

One, and Walkaway—be it in the guise of teacher, philosopher, poet, shaman, or leader (Fidyk, 2013b). Each image while distinct shares traits with one another—traits that are fluid, morphing into this or that—relationally enacted.

Poet Don Domanski (2002) writes:

> At poetry's centre there's the silence of a world turning. This is also found at the centre of a stone or at the axis of a tree. To my way of thinking, that silence is the main importance. Out of it come the manifestations, all the beings we call [W]ords. (p. 245)

Here is a new creation story: listening deeply reveals the gold (center). Find and embrace it (center) and Peace/Love—Silence is found. This treasure/Silence reveals insights, language, relations. Domanski adds that "presence is also a voice to listen to, to be influenced by" (p. 249). Presence as Witness is with us always already—felt and heard as the timbre of the cosmos. Through the practice of listening, tuning-in, proceeding by the inner ear, a method central to all teaching, we cultivate *empathos*. In-feeling—the ability to feel into other and respond to suffering. Listening is a mode of relationality that creates the possibility for learning from other, and it gives us a ground from which we might consider the specifically ethical potential of listening. Through the ear, we are tasked by the touch of "Words." Likewise, we can understand curriculum scholar David Smith's (2014) call to action. He urges us to engage "a new form of human conversation in which the abiding concern must be the alleviation of human suffering taken as a global responsibility" (p. 142). For some teachers, global responsibility might feel daunting, yet when imagined in relation to images of the Hero, Walkaway, and Elder, the task may find its natural embodiment.

One of the subtle features of a teacher as Wise One reflects her relationship to Silence and thus ways of respecting it within the curriculum, learning spaces, and the not-yet. As we saw with Poetry, Silence dwells in the intersection between an ontological position and epistemological practices. As the curriculum scholar Ted Aoki aptly explains, "The quality of life lived within the tensionality depends much on the quality of the *pedagogic being*" that the teacher *is* (Aoki, 1986, p. 161, emphasis added). Every teacher is confronted by this tension. What she chooses to do with it tells much about who she is and how she sees and so lives with the world.

Too often the teacher seeks to control, remove, or sublimate tension, revealing a dark side of teacher as Sage—as if it was not a valuable aspect of learning, as if Life was without its own resistance and force. Today pedagogy exists as a fluid dynamic whereby tensionality emerges from "indwelling in a zone between two curriculum worlds"—the worlds of "planned" and "lived" curriculum experiences (Aoki, 1986). The calling into presence of two curriculum forms, even though often singularly understood, allows one to understand more fully the pedagogic life of teachers. Aoki speaks of the quest we undertake for a transformation from the "is" to the "not-yet."

I highlight this tension so to better understand those students' lives—a similar quest awaiting many. They too lived in tensionality, one that prior to Gorgona was unspeakable. Because of the socioeconomic, political, and educational backgrounds of many of their families, the students were expected to assume positions of power, even corruption, and influence within the country. Many of the students had private bodyguards and took elaborate routes to and from school as protective measures, so they could not readily participate in the ordinary (team travel) or the spontaneous, and more than a few families had endured the kidnapping of members.

SILENCE AS GENERATIVE, CREATIVE, AND MEDITATIVE

Silence, perhaps in its most common form, has existed as forced silence. Traditionally, students (or captives) have been subdued, expected to be quiet when attending to assigned tasks—again, often in relation to negative forms of leadership. Such silence abides by external imposition typically as a form of discipline, order, and obedience. Silence too arises as a form of participation, membership, or even resistance, each of which cannot be read as a simple matter of power or lack of power, voice or lack of voice. Such forms of silence cannot be easily categorized as positive or negative in relation to the archetype because it all depends: each is dependent on culture, history, gender, class, and access to education (Fidyk, 2013a).

I flag the earlier example of Kaepernick, who, using intentional silence, protests social injustice (Kaepernick, *New York Times*, September 7, 2017). Just as students who see things differently and behave differently, from a set of "agreed" social and school norms, provoke subversion (Lees, 2012). Cheryl Glenn (2004) explains:

> Silence is too often read as simple passivity in situations where it has actually taken on an expressive power: when it denotes alertness and sensitivity, when it signifies attentiveness or stoicism, and particularly when it allows new voices to be heard. . . . Silence can deploy power; it can defer to power. It all depends. (p. 18)

"It all depends" acknowledges and respects the complexity of the factors relevant to silence, such as differentiating among types of silences, especially those that can be unfamiliar, uncertain, and paradoxical. However, where silence is understood as generative, creative, meditative, it can be a nourishing space in any learning place or daily practice, that is, space to know—in fresh, novel ways. Silence as a paradox figures prominently throughout Neruda's work. Here is a taste:

> Let me come to be still in your silence
> And let me talk to you with your silence
> That is bright as a lamp
> Simple, as a ring
> You are like the night
> With its stillness and constellations
> Your silence is that of a star
> As remote and candid. (Neruda, n.d.c)

"Mainstream contemporary educational systems . . . emphasize language as the only way we know or learn about this world," and that is simply not accurate (Zembylas & Michaelides, 2004, p. 209). Cultivated silence calls for a discipline from the inside out, a capacity to rest in one's authenticity, call it self, core, or soul, while simultaneously being in relation with the world. Recall the image of morning meditators. Its teaching manner cares for the well-being of youth and educators alongside the genuine inclusion and valuing of silence—a manner so strange to some that it has been called "unpedagogic" (Stern, 2012, p. 149). Sciacca suggested that this kind of silence "has a weight . . . that we don't find in any word: it is heavy with everything that we have lived, are living now and everything that we shall experience" (cited in Fiumara, 1990, p. 105).

> One time, near Antofagasta,
> between the squandered lives of men
> and the sandy circle
> of the pampas,
> not hearing or seeing anything, I stopped in nothingness:
> the air is vertical in the desert:
> there are no animals (not even flies)
> only the earth, like the moon, without roads,
> only the lower vastness of the planet,
> the dense kilometers of night and matter.
> There alone I sought the purpose of a land
> without men or wings, powerful,
> single in its reach, as if it had
> destroyed one by one those lives
> to impose its silence. (Neruda, 1971/1984, p. 57)

Conceived as primordial, prior to splitting into this and that, its multifarious positive and negative forms, Silence endures as an active experience. It is neither muteness nor mere absence of audible sound. Silence exists more like an "inner virtual condition" into which we can submerge and from which further understanding can emerge (Fiumara, 1990, p. 104). It is an "autonomous phenomenon" (Picard, 1948/2002, p. 15), "a force," a constitutive principle distinct from but associated with other forces, such as spirit and word, in the constitution of the human world (Dauenhauer, 1980, p. vii). That is, Silence is the *necessary* ground for building knowledge and relationships among self and others.

Silence is the "very foundation of learning," a truism few educators know, or practice, and so its restorative agent remains untapped (Caranfa, 2004, p. 211). In this way, "good practice" central to pedagogic encounters parallels "good practice" central to therapeutic encounters where the teacher embodies qualities and ways at the heart of a good psychotherapist/analyst. Good teaching shares much with good therapy. Directing both is the search for mutual understanding. Such mutuality is not symmetrical rather, it reflects relations that are two-way, embodying care and curiosity for the other. Such hermeneutic participation is a way of *being*-with, not a method or technique taught/learned in isolation. Akin to Domanski's discovery—'silence at the center of a turning world'—I once wrote about silence uncovered within my own pedagogic practice:

> We can be held together in a class first by the intent of the words, then by Silence itself. Often, after reading aloud in class a particularly affective piece of literature, Silence befalls us. It takes practice to let this Silence be, to not shatter its weight with an unnecessary question or comment. As I learned to let Silence breathe, I discovered [much] could arise from it. (Fidyk, 2008, p. 30)

While hiking in contorted, discontinuous lines through the lush Gorgona jungle, occasionally lapsing into small talk, it was as if something happened among us, *to us*—for that silence brought us into "living contact with the mysterious depths of ourselves, the creative spirit, the mysteries of love" (Lane, 2006, p. 96). Analogously, silence seems "the only thing that confronts us with our own life. It recapitulates it for us there, in that instant, entirely present" (Sciacca cited in Fiumara, 1990, p. 105).

"The emptiness of things—their inconsequence— . . . we sense this most deeply," writes Zwicky, "when we sense the fullness of the world's resonance in the thing. Nothing can echo with being unless it is emptied of itself"—that is, its subjectivity/-ies—its "I" state/s that keep us divided (p. 101). So as an educator, I cannot hear, sense, or meet a student without first being so settled in myself that my beliefs, views, and prejudices fall away, enabling me to "touch" her/them. Emptiness here, as in Buddhist thought, points to the true nature of things and encounters: our co-rising interconnectedness (see note 3). When Silence touches a teaching situation, be it public space or remote island, it enfolds those present in its energetic field—morphic, unified—experienced by some as a body sense, an opening to the way the Thing is heard and felt. Spellbound, it often prevents insignificant speech as a way to sustain itself.

"PHENOMENOLOGICAL EDGE," "RADICAL PRESENCE," AND "DEEP LISTENING"

Being surrounded by Gorgona's verdant rainforests, freshwater streams, and exotic fauna served to entrain us with the particularities of place. Often in silence, we were confronted by the initiatory address of things: humpback whales gathering to mate; screeching monkeys clamoring across clay roof tiles; lizards dropping down from palmately cleft leaves; and the lone sloth lumbering in branches high above. Because we were willing to attend to what poet Don McKay (2002) called "the phenomenological edge" (p. 60), and land "our attention on the particulars of this invitation, something happen" (derby, 2015, p. 2). Momentarily emptied of our human-centeredness, something addressed us from beyond our wanting and doing, beyond our constructs and categories. In this way, an ancient earthy wisdom emerged or at least seeded through slowing, noticing, and attending to something real, something relational, something ecological (Fidyk, 2017, p. 33).

Here some of us discovered that "meaningfulness always contains an absence as well as a presence," and sometimes in the absence of things, we become conscious of a presence that might have been long overlooked (Smith, 1999, p. 71). In this way "silence is as much as declaration" (p. 71). While a teacher with access to the Wise One archetype may create space for silence's "radical presence," whereby at any moment it may break forth, nothing, however, in the previous moment guarantees its arrival (O'Reilley, 1998).

I recall this happening when a student, excited to share his encounter with a boa, met me on the trail to breakfast one morning. He described the meeting, but the words failed to capture his body sense or *somatic synaesthesia* of what was experienced. Face fallen, frustration seeped in as the telling fell short and his voice dropped off. He paused and grew quiet. Eventually, that quietness transformed into a generative silence. He looked up as he felt me listening— *silently in touch with him.* We continued to stand there for a few more minutes, neither of us speaking, morning light reaching tentatively through palm fronds, until he gently said: "It was like this." I smiled and nodded, both of us reluctant to say anything more.

"Presence to another can be this informal"—even if the other is snake or sunrise (O'Reilley, 1998, p. 24). As Zwicky (1992) writes, "To be open to the world is to experience presence" (p. 209). It implies deep and intentional listening. And it implies a willingness to touch and be touched. In order to "practice radical presence—to come home to your heart and listen deeply to others who look for you there"—someone must have first listened to you (O'Reilley, 1998, p. 16).

As the inner ear is to the body, listening is to silence. A vibrational world of attunement and touch—a world that begins quite literally during the seventh week of life when the middle chambers of the embryonic human's ears become functionally alive. "The most significant aspect of this development is that a sense of stability has become part of the *becoming human being*. The embryo can *now balance itself* within the womb. The inner ear communicates with structures that provide static equilibrium throughout life" (Merker, 2000, p. 23, italics added). Listening, balance, living with tensionality, dwelling as midline of both vertical and horizontal axes—hyphen, flesh and "keeping oneself equal with"—this occurrence is a "fortuitous gift of heritage"—passed down through our early aquatic life forms (p. 23).

Recent studies report that at the beginning of the third trimester, the float-ing child exhibits selective attention, tuning out that which is annoying or disturbing. "Three months before it leaves its water world, a human being is listening" (Merker, 2000, p. 24). "Listening," describes Dr. Gardner, of the Huntington Hearing and Speech Center, New York, is "a state when one does not know one is listening . . . one is spontaneous, no longer conscious of self . . . it is a form of ego loss when there is no barrier between you and someone else" (p. 25). Listening happens when we are attentive, attuned, yet alert: awake. That is, ego loss, not fragmentation or disassociation as is often the case. The radical difference between "tuning out" and "tuning in." When we choose responsibly "to receive and understand an earth message of some kind; Listening is a conscious act" (p. 28). This the Wise One knows.

Composer and artist Pauline Oliveros (2006) defines listening as the act of giving "attention to sound or sounds or to perceive with the ear, to hear with thoughtful attention, to consider seriously" (p. xxii). Listening takes place in the "auditory cortex and is based on the experience of the waveforms trans-mitted by the ear to the brain" (p. xxii). We associate and categorize based on the range and depth of our experience, a process that continues throughout one's lifetime. "Acoustic space is where time and space merge as they are articulated by sound" (Bandt cited in Oliveros, 2005, p. xxiii).

While "deep" has to do with complexity and boundaries, or edges beyond ordinary or habitual understandings, coupled with "listening," "deep listen-ing" for Oliveros means "learning to expand the perception of sounds to include the whole space/time continuum of sound"—encountering the vast-ness and complexities as much as possible (p. xxiii). Such focus, she says, "should always return to, or be within the whole of the space/time continuum (context)" (p. xxiii). Such expansion means that one is always already con-nected to the whole of the ecosystem and beyond.

Listening as a receptive, attentive act when one is "no longer conscious of self" shares kinship with intuition—"an instinctive, immediate seeing"—permitting access to images that emerge deep from within the collective unconscious (Jung cited in van den Berk, 2012, p. 93; Fidyk, 2014, p. 14). Zwicky (2012) describes intuition as "immediate awareness of resonance . . . sustained attention to abstract and concrete images—kinaesthetic, aural, tactile, emotional, visual, and olfactory gestalts an ontological attention, and the perception of *what is there in ways that calculative reason cannot [make up]*" (p. 27, emphasis in original). She suggests that the lyrical is a kind of "intuition" (p. 28) and offers other poets' descriptions of the ways the lyrical as a kind of intuition serves to enrich our lives (pp. 22–26). Neruda (1968/2008) does the same:

> Here I have a leaf,
> an ear, a whisper,
> a thought:
> I am going to live again,
>
> the roots hurt me,
> the hair,
> the mouth smiles at me:
> I rise
> because the sun has risen.
> Because the sun has risen. (pp. 56–57)

A teacher as Wise One trusts such insight, direct perception of truth, immediate cognition, or "spiritual perception"— a form of contemplation, "a noun of action stemming from '*look at, consider*,' from *in-* 'at, on'" (intuition). Intuition moves "*in* tune with being, hearing and echoing the music and heartbeat of being" (Bringhurst, 2007, emphasis added); likewise, it acts as a "voice" that "embodies being" (Lee, 1998, cited in Zwicky, 2012, p. 23). It inspires us to utter names "which its subjects . . . intone if they stood to sing" (Lilburn, 1999, cited in Zwicky, 2012, p. 23); and it embodies "inspiration, divination, rapture" (Gustafson, 1987, cited in Zwicky 2012, p. 26).

"Essentially," intuition "means to be aware, to answer the call from life itself, to practice the veneration of its numerous forms" (Domanski, 2006, in Zwicky 2012, p. 22); it presents an "irresistible urge to acknowledge the awe [felt] in the presence of creation" (Lee, 1998, cited in Zwicky 2012, p. 23). How might the teacher as Sage, Strong Poet, or Wise One encourage intuition as an equally valid form of consciousness as sensing across all curricula? (See Grandstaff's section on "perceiving function.") One looks inward, while the other outward, yet both are indispensable to our creativity and to our be(com)ing.

PEDAGOGY AS CREATIVE ENDEAVOR, AS "DEEP PLAY," AS "DEEP PEDAGOGY"

When we attend to images, feelings, and words anew, it is a creative act. As Zen teacher Toni Packer (2007) shares, "There is nothing more miraculous than thorough attention, no matter what the activity may be" (p. 77). "Attend" directs focus toward something, to listen; its Latin root *attendere* means "to stretch and to wait," eventually becoming the Latin verb *tenere*, meaning "to hold and contain" (Ayto, 1993). In its continued transformation, attend took the meaning of "caring for and to be present with," suggesting a *waiting* and *stretching* that could be applied to the idea of the softening ego consciously extending toward a relationship with the unconscious. Through such attention, educators might discover that Silence itself is a creative act and can arouse creativity in kind for when the mind or voice grows quiet, a door opens to the unknown. Here Things can emerge, as the stories of the student and boa and the meditators attest.

"In its creative function," writes philosopher Gemma Fiumara, "silence basically represents a way of being *with* the interlocutor; it indicates . . . a proposed interaction, an invitation to the development of a time-space in which to meet, or clash, in order to share in the challenge of growth" (p. 101). "Everything is changed in real meeting," and "real meeting" includes disagreement—"clash" (Buber, 1999, pp. 242–243). That is, we must take the other in their dynamic existence, in their specific potentiality, even when they hold a view or value contrary to our own. As Buber describes, "That is the hidden, for in the present lies hidden what *can become*. His potentiality makes itself felt to me as that which I would most confirm" (p. 243, emphasis added).

Mary Catherine Bateson (1994) extends this understanding of creativity:

> I would call [a creative act] a godlike act, except that the word evokes, for too many, a sense of distance and dominance, while seeing anew is a kind of intimacy; I would call it childlike, if it were not important to avoid blocking learning with the reminders of all that was onerous in childhood. In the ordinary creativity of moving through the world, we are both gods and children. (p. 10)

As this interpretation suggests, there is a spiritual basis to attendance, a humility in waiting upon the emergence of a pattern from the world. The willingness to assimilate what has been touched, seen, or heard, "a setting of things side by side," draws other life into increasingly inclusive definitions of the self (Zwicky, 2003, p. L7). The emergence of the self, as a transpersonal and ethical potentiality, expands and enriches through deepening connections with the archetypal—experiences that reach beyond the individual yet are nevertheless an innate part of all human nature. Depth psychology and Islamic scholar Tom Cheetham (2003) describes it thus: "The archetypal creative act is not based on Power but on Love . . . and to create is to Love" (p. 152).

Pedagogy as a creative endeavor shares "a commitment to acknowledging, mourning, and celebrating what-is—its non-, its extra-, and its fully human dimensions" (Zwicky, 2008, p. 86). That is, a creative or poetic orientation from and reciprocally to the world does not aim at reductive explanations to fit the "complexity, polyphony, and ineffability of what-is into human constructs" (derby, 2015, p. 5). Its primary gesture is a disciplined act of attending to things, of tarrying, and such an understanding is "ontologically robust" even as it points beyond the human (Zwicky, 2008, p. 86). Such pointing calls upon analyst D. W. Winnicott (1971/2005) for whom "the creative impulse" belonged to both humans and animals when "feeling that life is real or meaningful" (p. 93). Recognizing the animating aspect of the cosmos, he argued that creativity is universal: "It belongs to being alive" (p. 91). Underscoring both is Whitehead's first principle,"Creativity," whereby, "the many become one, and are increased by one" (1978, p. 21). The whole aim of the universe is "to generate increasingly complex individual experiences: but such novel uniqueness can only take place through increasing intricacy and breadth of community" (Keller, 1986, p. 183). It is the horizon of existence, not the verticality, which brings us home, revealing communion with Things (Fidyk, 2017, p. 34).

Relation is primary. It is all about the becoming, the being, and the relatedness of the real things of which the world is made. In this light, creativity and so relations can be understood as the principal ethical task.

"Ontological understanding," Zwicky (2003) explains, "is rooted in the perception of patterned resonance in the world," and "philosophy, practiced as a setting of things side by side until the similarity dawns, is a form of ontological appreciation" (p. L7). Such ontological understanding and appreciation is central to inquiry-based learning—with its poetic, hermeneutic, and somatic sensibilities—and together redirect education axiomatically toward kinship, interconnectedness, ancestry, empathy, humility, and wonder—paradoxically, toward *depth pedagogy* or *deep pedagogy*.

By extension, we are confronted with the ethical implications that arise from this positioning. That is, in 'a setting of things side by side,' we perceive patterns of what-is and thereby we recognize the significance of each element, its singularities, to the overall gestalt. Like life within the rainforest, it exists in "an interactive and polymorphous form" and only through such recognition might we revise our beliefs, actions, and so values (derby, 2015, p. 15; Fidyk, 2017, p. 34).

Archetypal connectivity and creativity call upon the gods. A creative act accompanied by playfulness evokes Hermes; creativity conjoined with eros and relatedness calls forth Aphrodite; and, a creative act conjoined with ingenuity calls upon Hephaestus. Yet, despite individual influence, Hermes, God of Borders and Boundaries, Liminality, and Play, negotiates the creative tension between the *eros* (emotions, feelings, hopes) and *logos*—analytics, procedures, grammar—aspects of education. Relationships with 'both gods and children' nurture, for example, the inner child —in student and teacher—who is "a source of energy, playfulness, and fun, as well as providing a challenge to the adult in our students" (Lindley, 1993, p. 72).

Remember, the bipolar aspect of the archetype requires that the teacher must have access to her inner child so that the student can have access to his inner teacher. The teacher–student dyadic interactions require the "inner tension between the states of being a knowledgeable adult and an unknowing child" for reciprocity (Guggenbühl-Craig, 1971, p. 104). Perhaps this uncommon perception of the "ties that bind" teacher and student offers a fresh understanding of the familiar while rejuvenating the teacher and so the whole teaching-and-learning-encounter (Fidyk, 2016a, 2016b). Bateson offers us this relevant metaphor: "Looking, listening, and learning offer the modern equivalent of moving through life as a pilgrimage" (1994, p. 11).

As a pilgrim, the teacher must orient as if a newcomer to a strange or foreign land. They would be well served if curious, wonder-filled, and questioning. With eyes, ears, and touch eager to read and know that particular world. Teaching with this orientation entices her "children within" thereby permitting the students' "adults within" to appear. As such the two are invited to move more fluidly than the rigidity that currently characterizes learning where assessment and accountability tend to harden rather than soften teachers' edges. In 'life as a pilgrimage' we are invited to journey, sometimes with companionship, sometimes with solitude. It means to tarry, to sojourn with a caring and receptive attitude. The willingness to do what needs to be done—the pedagogic good—is rooted in attention to what is. That is, the dyadic interactions of teacher–student as complexity-and-context-sensitive ought to be characterized by compassion. For the teacher who can *see through* the personal, acknowledging it as part of the collective and transpersonal, real understanding can unfold.

Compassion, etymologically *compatior*, means "a bearing together, a suffering-with." As such, it is not a technique nor a skill; instead, it is "both process and attitude" (Orange, 2010, p. 115). As process, compassion is akin to emotional understanding (Orange, 1995), the dialogic process of undergoing the situation with the other (Gadamer, 1960/1991), and coming-to-an-understanding of the emotional situation within the relational system that we experience together, a system that gradually changes. A compassionate attitude, which is not always meant to be kind or gentle—indeed, it may challenge or contradict or introduce alternative perspectives—enables otherwise unknown and impossible forms of experiencing (Orange, 2010).

Here the best care for students may be founded in felt observation or contemplation. To be attuned to learning, teachers as Wise Ones, Elders, Pilgrims, and Strong Poets develop an authentic and deliberate kind of attention. Such attention does not imply that something must be done; rather, it emphasizes a profound respect of attending deeply beyond the sensate. As for reconnection to the gods—Hermes, Zeus, Aphrodite, and Eros, to name a few (Dobson, 2008a, 2008b, 2009; Fidyk, 2009, 2010; Lindley, 1993, 2006; Mayes, 2005,

2017; Moore & Gillette, 1990; Neville, 2012; Wakefield, 2016)—they possess numerous gifts from which both teacher and student can benefit.

According to the educator and analyst Daniel Lindley (1993), the "*ultimate sign of successful teaching*" plays out in the following sequence (p. 126): a student is puzzled by a discrepancy in a concept not understood or within an occurrence in a story. The teaching proceeds; the student listens, talks, writes. The problem arises again, in a varied form. The student continues to work at it, but then at a certain point the student ingests the new concept. At that moment it ceases to be new. If the new idea is inherently resonant with the student's nature, true to human nature in general, then the newness will disappear insensibly into familiarity. In this way, the student becomes the teacher.

Pedagogically, play in this form is not something one does; rather, it is something that one *has to do* or is *called to do*, joining serious endeavor and playful creation. "Deep play"—that which is necessary for all outward creativity—Diane Ackerman (1999) calls "transcendent play"; "a deeper form of play, akin to rapture and ecstasy, that humans relish, even require to feel whole" (p. 12). "It contains uncertainty, illusion, an element of make-believe or fantasy, and allows one to take risks, or explore new roles" (p. 14). In our most positive portrayals, teacher as Sage, Elder, Walkaway, and Wise One must not only make space for play but also create the very milieu that hosts it and know when to let their inner child appear.

THE SEA, LIMINALITY, AND THE GODS

> Ocean, if you were to give, a measure, a ferment, a fruit
> of your gifts and destructions, into my hand,
> I would choose your far-off repose, your contour of steel,
> your vigilant spaces of air and darkness,
> and the power of your white tongue,
> that shatters and overthrows columns,
> breaking them down to your proper purity. (Neruda, n.d.a)

Learning to dwell in difficult situations or zones of tensionality—ambiguity, uncertainty, and risk taking—creates a sense of faith in a particular kind of Presence, one that is not readily named or described. For some it is easier to deny, repress, or ignore such challenges rather than being with what on the surface appears troublesome, problematic, or useless. However, when one has acquired access to or developed a steadfast relationship with Presence, the times when contact is lost become increasingly intolerable. Nevertheless, when dwelling in those difficult places, there may come a moment

> when the wholeness of the phenomenon bursts upon you. When that moment
> occurs, an intense joy accompanies it, a moment in which you are caught up

in the wonder of the thing itself. And there is also this pause, this pregnant point, when you and the phenomenon itself—at this moment of interwoven, participatory consciousness—are suspended in time in a state of dynamic tension. (Buhner, 2004, p. 187)

After glimpsing such wholeness, we might experience a shift in consciousness—a newness that endures until the next glimpse.

This transformation happens in the badgering and bothering, and correcting and grading; it happens as well in the ground of Silence. It happens in good teaching where members know their individual attention contributes to what might emerge on any given day, when they are willing to be vulnerable and present to what is. Embracing what arises through inquiry, students' interests and questions, contributes to the development or deepening of trust, courage, and confidence not only within students and teachers but also within pedagogical spaces—places that can then invite and hold more of the same energetic. This field or the field effect in pedagogy (Fidyk, 2010, 2016a, 2016b, 2017) is rarely discussed in education except perhaps in terms of the transference and counter-transference—"the exchange of unconscious wishes; the displacement of our first love onto figures of authority, and the transposition of symbolic equivalences of old and repressed conflicts onto the understanding of new situations" (Britzman, 2006, p. 179)—as in the work of psychoanalytically oriented curriculum scholars (Britzman, 1998, 2006, 2009, 2015; Boldt & Salvio, 2006; Doll, 2000, 2011, 2017; Farley, 2014; Felman, 1987, 1992; Grumet, 1988; Mayes, 2010, 2017; Pitt, 2003; Robertson, 1996; Taubman, 2012; Todd, 1997a, 1997b, 2003).

As field theory and somatic resonance propose, there is a collective knowing already at play—a pattern laid down transtemporally and transgenerationally—as dynamic, as relational, and paradoxically, as both gift and loss. Biologist Rupert Sheldrake (1995/2012) said it simply: "Memory is inherent in nature." That is, there is a field resonance as collective and cumulative memory among members of a species that is passed preconception trans-time-and-space. Students and teachers carry forth their fields of history, as members of the human species, and of particular familial lines, that act as memory of previous existence tagged with cultural/ethnic influences and the impact of epigenetics. These fields and lines affect learning (see Fidyk, 2016a, 2016b). The content of familial fields can make it more difficult to break or change particular patterns, be it affectionate feelings or hostile ones. Here we see the analogous nature to transference: As Freud (1970) put it, "a new edition" of an old problem appears wherein the youth projects issues from childhood onto the teacher (p. 462). Whether or not, the student is released from this entanglement depends not on his "intellectual insight" but rather on his relationship with the teacher (p. 453). Again not entirely, a flowing from the student (traditional view of transference), nor a flowing into him (the counter-transference); rather, "within the transference, [there is] a certain limit, a certain threshold [that] is never crossed and always transgressed—the porosity of the mucous membranes" (Irigaray, 1991, p. 113). It is an indeterminate space-time; a third space, a mucous space, a shared space where each is involved. For Sheldrake, all of nature—cells, organisms, species—emerges through formative causation and seeks out fields of somatic resonance. This Neruda (n.d.b) knew, as evidenced in the sea's affect upon things:

> *Naiad*:   cut your body into turquoise pieces, they will bloom resurrected in the kitchen. This is how you become everything that lives.

Let us return to Gorgona—.

During the day we hike, snorkel, and attend to what normally would go unnoticed: coconuts audibly decomposing; a python curled in the sun; and cutter ants carrying puzzle pieces of green, striding in delicate, ordered lines. After one particularly grueling hike, several miles through undulating, slippery mud paths, when the roar and scent of the Sea reached us, before it did, we quickened our pace and poured from the jungle onto miles of beach. Dropping water bottles, boots, and what clothes we still wore, we threw our bodies against the needle sharp waves, and into the ferocious undercurrents, surrendering to the Sea.

Where are these students today? What lives chose them? What fates were overturned, sidestepped? Did the Sea leave its mark on them as it did on me?

Or Poetry? Tugging on their memories as something older and grander than themselves—like the traces of salty, amniotic waters that run in our mnemonic veins?

> . . . here I shall be again the movement
> of the water,
> of its wild heart,
> here I shall be both lost and found—
> here I shall be perhaps both stone and silence. (Neruda as
> cited in Poirot, 1990, p. 104)

Ancient and primal, the Sea is "our mother of mothers, the Great Round within whose fluid containment life began and from whose fertile precincts the first bold pioneers scuttled out upon the sand" (Martin, 2010, p. 36). The Sea, for many, represents the meeting place of image and instinct, soul body and corporeal body, where the imaginal strives for depth, resonance, and texture. This meeting place symbolizes, like Hermes, and the hyphen, the borderland, the betwixt and between—of the spiritual and natural worlds—and the times of the forgotten and the not-yet. The symbolic significance of the sea corresponds to that of the "Lower Ocean"—"the waters in flux, the transitional and mediating agent between the non-formal (air and gases) and the formal (earth and solids) and, by analogy, between life and death" (Cirlot, 2014, p. 281). As colleague, Mark Grandstaff (2019) advises, "Let the Muses and the Gods guide you on the path of this unknown sea and you will find authenticity in living an individuated life" (see Grandstaff appendix B: Jungian Types).

Liminality is "a space that invites anomaly, and relishes ambiguity" (Neilsen, 1998, p. 273); a place where we "perceive patterns in new ways, find sensuous openings into new understandings, fresh concepts, wild possibilities," a place where we "subvert the ordinary and see the extraordinary" (p. 274). Where the liminal and the lyric meet is a place of play, fluidity, and imagination. It is a means of connection: Call it skin. As poet Jane Hirshfield (1997) writes:

> The liminal is not opposite to, but the necessary companion of, identity and particularity—a person who steps outside her usual position falls away from any singular relationship to others and into oneness with the community as a whole. Within the separateness of liminality, separateness itself is remade . . . entire societies, as well as individuals, at times enter the condition of threshold for renewal. (p. 204)

We are reminded of the necessity of dropping subjectivities (not in their singularities but in their separateness and divisiveness), of risking, and of bringing the child and the adult together as "equals," within teaching-and-learning spaces.

An example of bringing the child and adult together can be found in the way Apollo regards baby Hermes—his fury and amusement at the newborn's skill in not only stealing his sacred cattle but also eating two of them. The baby feels as able as the adult. Equality in position must be obtained between adult and inner child for the adult to be able to feel the child's energy and so be renewed by it. While our remembered child is part of our story, it is not the same as the child whose energy we seek in teaching—this energy stems from the archetype.

What Lindley calls the "archetypal foundation of third-stage teaching"— and that "foundation is in a paradox, a combination of opposites: it is in the *wise child*: ultimately, the *divine child*" (1993, p. 110). This wise child does not need to be cared for because it can care for itself; it is a child, yet it knows all there is to know. Its wisdom does not diminish its openness and its excitement. It is precisely this combination that sustains the teacher. For many, openness is gradually replaced with wisdom—"the old become oracular and distant—like Zeus" (p. 110). But this change will not bring fulfillment. Teaching can be fulfilling only "if the joy of the new is as present as the joy of the known" (p. 111).

Hermes's significance for any teacher is that he stands "between the child and the adult, between impulse and skill, between the mortals and the immortals" (Lindley, 1993, p. 111). Relevant here are three aspects of Hermes that inform teaching:

(1) He stands where teachers stand; he stands in liminal space; (2) He is a trickster, and so knows how to seem unknowing while actually knowing; and (3) [H]e is a messenger, a crosser of borders, bringing words from Olympus [which] . . . holds both the *logos* of ideas and understandings (represented by Apollo) and the *eros* of faith, hope, and love represented by Hera, Demeter, and Aphrodite. Hermes moves between all these realms. (p. 111)

Deep pedagogy happens in the liminal—on the hyphen, as flesh, the border between adulthood and childhood, between knowing and unknowing, between certainty and mystery—and the teacher, her-self can embody these traits. These traits intersect with qualities associated with the teacher as Strong Poet, Walkaway, and Elder, for it is in their presence where something unexpected can break forth.

Psychologically mature teachers consciously influenced by these archetypal images dwell in the territory between order and chaos—where students, especially adolescents, live. It is here where greatest growth occurs—through meeting and clashing; trusting and suspecting—if the latter is done with conscious intention or reflection. As Lindley so playfully puts it: "The trick (the trickster's task) is to stay on this boundary (liminality again). Hermes in our story steals the cattle (chaos) but invents and masters the lyre (order). *Teachers, too, must do both*" (p. 119, emphasis added).

Known as Demeter, Artemis, as well as the Egyptian Isis, Babylonian Ishtar, and Buddhist Kwan-yin, the feminine principle of the cosmos—receptive, fertile, nurturing—the Great Mother is the ground of existence both literally and metaphorically. She is associated with intuition, the body, and feeling; and, she is known for caring, yielding, holding, mirroring, and equilibrating. Too much and she becomes smothering; too little and she becomes neglecting. Like a good therapist or a "good enough mother,"[8] the teacher's ability to balance the energies within herself and to hold what arises in the pedagogic space enables students to explore aspects of their own becoming as well as ideas, humor, and imagination (Winnicott, 1953). Qualities that, practically speaking, can be interpreted as ways or methods vital to the twenty-first-century "classroom": the *method of ideas*, the *way of humor*, and the *method of imagination*.

Just as the sea held us, allowing my own experimentation, when students feel held, there is trust and a sense of safety, allowing their own experimentation. Likewise, Winnicott (1971/2005) believed that creativity required special containment and care, and "*only if reflected back* [original emphasis]" could it become part of the organized individual personality (p. 86). While traditionally associated with the feminine or maternal, and perhaps still biasing teaching as a feminized profession, trust mediates learning. Consistent across models of trust provided by caregivers during infancy and childhood, to the "ongoing patterns of trust that are affected by life experiences including trauma, the ability to trust is essential to all aspects of life and functioning" (Nader, 2006, p. 126). Early attachments prepare the ground for later relationships and aid the child to "develop self-confidence, self-control, self-awareness, and awareness of the emotions of others" (p. 126). Our role in *loco parentis* is just that. All educators would be well served to take this to heart.

While the ethos of the pedagogic space can be tilted when only one archetypal parent is present, when they appear together, such as the Great Mother and the Great Father, as equal partners sharing in authoritative teaching, such teachers are known for their high expectations and high care—cognitively challenging yet emotionally safe. Available care and positive self-regard foster the development of flexible problem-solving skills, emotion regulation patterns, and an expectation of success in the face of adversity.

These teachers insist that their students attain their personal best regarding a certain issue or question, and they give of themselves to this process. They relate lovingly and authentically with their students; they are in touch with their own emotions and feelings; they trust their intuitions and the spontaneity of images, associations, and ideas. Most important, they encourage their students to create opportunities for them to access and cultivate their own intuition, feelings, emotions, and creative urges. They assess in ways that are trustworthy and varied, non-punitive, and always valuable to the student's ongoing development as a full human being (Mayes, 2010, pp. 105–130).

> Whole ecosystems, untouched by sunlight, flourish in the sea just as networks of accumulated experience flourish in the psyche, enhancing the waters regardless of our knowledge of their existence. . . . Tidal currents course through our deeps and shallows, yielding to the rhythmic pull of moon and sun. The undulations of our myriad intensities combine in ever-changing patterns reflected on our surfaces, just as the patterns of wave trains—"intermingling, overtaking, passing, or sometimes engulfing one another"—are endlessly reconfigured over the face of the sea. (Carson cited in Martin, 2010, p. 36)

Like sunlight filtered through the depths of the sea, that necessary and that unnoticed, we are in continuous energetic relationship with all Things. Here the teacher attunes to the whole class and to each student (of that group) with her care—adjusting tone and tact, an implication of touch, to the fecundity of each case. Learning to attune to our breath and its subtle, yet radical, influence on our health and functioning, we can gain awareness of the tangible, yet invisible, world. Just as we unconsciously attune to our mothers' heartbeat and voice, breath imprints the rhythmic exchange of bringing the other—image, sound, animal, idea—into our presence like water mingling with sand, two different elements mixing, borrowing, giving life to each other.

This act reflects the pedagogical attunement that subsumes teacher and learner when they fall into a shared joy of discovery—that erotic[9] impulse of curiosity, wonder, and creativity—when applying imaginings and ideas to new contexts and lives. Having conscious access to the distinguishing characteristics of archetypal images that the teacher can draw upon makes the possibility of attuning to different students and situations, even youth who are challenging, avoidant, and resistant, an actuality. For example, teachers who are unconsciously too much Mother would benefit from developing traits that define Hermes, Zeus, or Apollo as well as features that are associated with Athena, Artemis, or Aphrodite (Fidyk, 2009, 2010).

BEAUTY, DIALOGUE, AND TRUST

Coupled with the acquisition of new skills and knowledge that are inherent in this creative process, teachers and students alike commit to the rhythmic sway where the questions asked or the acts imagined govern what follows. In this way, we embody the initial awakening, the discipline, and the fruition on a more developed or more complex level than previously, whereby we experience the principle of movement from within: "The discovery is made by ourselves, the discipline is self-discipline, and the fruition is the outcome of our own initiative" (Whitehead, 1929/1967, p. 39). The decisive prompting, alike in science, ethics, and literature, is the sense of value, the sense of importance. It can take the form of wonder, reverence, worship, or tumultuous desire for merging personality in something beyond itself—the singular within the collective. For Whitehead, the most acute form of this force is "the sense of beauty, the aesthetic sense of realized perfection" (p. 40). Such perfection is found in the fullest expression of thing as Thing!

In what ways did the Sea, its movement, sounds, and silences, tug on our choices, responses, and responsibilities, perhaps taking years to surface, and then surfacing in the night, unnamed? Not unlike Neruda's desire:

> Is the Sea there? Tell it to come in.
> Bring me
> the great bell, one of the green race.
> Not that one, the other one, the one that has
> a crack in its bronze mouth,
> and now, nothing more, I want to be alone
> with my essential Sea and the bell.
> I don't want to speak for a long time,
> Silence! I still want to learn,
> I want to know if I exist. (Neruda, 2002b , p. 111)

During the evenings, we would gather on the shore and swim with the phosphorescent plankton, gently cupping the glowing orbs, enchanted by their light. Eventually, small groups of students formed. Some broke off and trailed along the beach, others sat on the rocks till curfew, while others plotted night escapes from assigned sleeping quarters. And some, some continue to linger in my memory—part of the present not only the past.

They shared glimpses of their inner worlds, hopes, desires, fears, all of which revealed them intimately. Even their shadows showed through the seemingly disjointed and difficult-to-understand dreams, stories, and fantasies. They seemed to be "leaning out for love," even the most difficult youth (Karen, 1994). The openness of the field trip's "unpedagogic" structure softened the teacher-student boundaries, permitting dialogue, despite the riskiness of that path.

As trauma studies repeatedly attest, the grounding of a secure therapeutic relationship (established safety and trust) is *the* factor in treatment. As I have learned pedagogically and therapeutically, the establishment of security, safety (trust), and a climate of empathy always has been of central importance for students to risk themselves in relationship or in learning (one and the same). Attachment theorists espouse the critical role of responsiveness and empathic attunement in the psychotherapeutic relationship.

A secure base arises out of the responsiveness and attunement provided by the therapist [educator]. Attunement is, by its very nature, non-controlling, following rather than leading, affective rather than instrumental. It is "aimless" in the sense that it cannot legislate in advance for what will emerge from the playful and spontaneous encounter between therapist and patient. . . . You cannot prescribe what is going to happen in a session. . . . What can be prescribed are the conditions favorable to secure base. (Holmes, 2001, p. 50)

I suggest the same is true within the pedagogic relationship—some students unknowingly seek to acquire, and others to maintain, conditions favorable to a secure base. While bound by mandated curricula, the ways teachers enact and assess learning outcomes have much flexibility and room for creativity yet often become limited by the perceived need for control, as seen in the negative side of Mother and Sage. By revitalizing practice through archetypal reflectivity, teachers can uncover, discover, even recover relations as primary—interpersonally and intrapsychically—and host *the art of pedagogy* in diverse learning spaces, be they public, urban, wild, etc.

Despite the shared root of hostility and hospitality, *hostis*—meaning "enemy" or "guest"—the latter continues to be at stake. As I discovered with students on Gorgona, it is only through intentional effort to meet the other that we develop beyond our repetitions and secret fears. When we step out of our habits of thought, we are met by the unexpected. Dialogue "implies the necessity of the unforeseen and its basic element is surprise, the surprising mutuality" (Buber, 1999, p. 190). However, teaching-and-healing relationships share the requisite asymmetry of parenting and, by their very nature, never unfold into complete mutuality. When mutuality is sought, we see the dark side of the Sage or Elder. When, or perhaps if, an educator grasps with the hermetic eye of a Shaman or Walkaway the "buried, latent unity of the suffering soul, which can be done only if he enters as a partner in a person-to-person relationship, but never through the observation and investigation of an object," this hosting illustrates a form of grace (Buber, 1999, p. 179). Grace "for which we must always be prepared but on which we can never count" (p. 178).

The I-You relation, as described, is "intimate, surprising, risky, and creates a genuine We" (Orange, 2010, p. 22). It cannot always be fully reciprocal; it need not be constant; and it is not mystical. And yet the words that arose between some students and me "[came] to life in the We of speech" (p. 22), "the communal speaking that begins in the midst of speaking to one another" (Buber, 1999, p. 106). The We, "the living community of the past and present, depends on language, always ontologically present" (Orange, 2010, p. 22). In this way, speaking is touch, intimacy, the "personal making present" required for real contact (Buber, 1999, p. 79):

The actual other who meets me in such a way that my soul comes in contact with his as with something that it is not and that it cannot become. My soul does not and cannot include the other, and yet can approach the other in the most real contact. (Buber, 1999, p. 56)

In such dialogue, we fell into ourselves and wondered wildly about the ways of the living and the dead—that is the archetypal, metaphoric, and epi/genetic lineages. At times ghosts surfaced for even they need to be heard. Be it from atrocities in Colombia during the 1990s or those of this century, "the process of remembering and truth telling are critical to the healing process" (Herman, 1992, cited in Muller, 2010, p. 42). In the great stream of reciprocal sharing of knowledge, when possible, "the genuine We, which, where it fulfills itself, embraces the dead who once took part in colloquy and now take part in it through what they have handed down to posterity," their traces lingering in our fields (p. 107). There is a circle of touching and touched; and similarly, there is a circle of seeing and seen—a reciprocal insertion and intertwining of one with the other—enfolded together as one.

Language became richest where "out of understanding each other, genuine dialogue 'unfolds'" (p. 150). When it did, it became "the radical condition of learning and of knowledge" (Felman, 1987, p. 83). As such dialogue refers to the capacity of Other (teacher, parent, therapist) to bring into the symbolic realm aspects of the youth's subjectivity that have previously been unarticulated. The subject, paradoxically, can become a subject only through dialogue—linguistic touch! Language too includes the "inner word"—dialogue with self, including splinter selves, imaginal figures, and the witness alongside the layers and veils of the "outer word," which also includes the Witness or Self (Buber, 1988, p. 102). "The dialogic word may even be a silent sitting or walking together" (p. 258). However, dialogue loses its defining purpose and form—that is, engagement between-two or more bodies—when it is practiced with negative projection as when teachers and parents force their own demands, consciously and unconsciously, upon youth.

Living with integrity, a potential gift of engaging in archetypal reflectivity, demands accepting visions of our greatness and our smallness, our loves and our hates, our dreams and our shames. When we accept our own limitations and shortcomings—both our personal shadows and those of the archetypal images, it becomes easier to engage in open inquiry and to see wonder, risk, and err as part of the learning rhythm. As symbolized by the hermeneutic circle in H.-G. Gadamer's hands, the back and forth of question and response becomes the mutual interplay of learning from each other in coming to an understanding—as witnessed through the images of the Strong Poet, Elder, and Wise One. A "conversation," for him, "is always a kind of living together and as such it has its incontestable and unreachable priority" (Gadamer & Hahn, 1997, pp. 403–404). Gadamer's version of Socratic "recollection"—knowing meant remembering—was "not only that of the individual soul but always that of the 'spirit who would like to unite us'—we who are a conversation" (Michelfelder & Palmer, 1989, p. 110). "Spirit" here is akin to creativity and divinity—the organizing principle of existence.

Whether we encounter a sunset, a text, or a person, the process of understanding is intermediary. In any case, we meet the other precisely as other. And "everything is changed in real meeting" (Buber, 1999, p. 242). The primary direction of experience is not solely inward; rather, its very nature thrusts us into the world. It forces us to come to terms with the not-us/not-I, yet once the concept or situation is met, whereby embodied consciousness expands in order to comprehend, the movement is reiterated. Experience then implies the interweave of *both* poles—self/Self and other/Other, inward and outward, subjective and objective, visible and invisible—*and* the intermediate between our inner realities and the shared reality/-ies of the world that is external—the other flesh to our flesh, pulsating as part of the universe's perpetual becoming.

"REAL WORK," "MISENCOUNTERS," AND TOUCH

Philosopher Simone Weil (1952) offers a fitting comment on the circuitous revisiting of my teaching encounter on Gorgona:

In our sense perceptions, if we are not sure of what we see we change our position while looking, and what is real becomes evident. In the inner life, time takes
the place of space. With time we are altered, and, if as we change we keep our
gaze directed towards the same thing, in the end illusions are scattered and the
real becomes visible. This is on condition that the attention be a looking and not
an attachment. (p. 174)

Weil, like the other philosophers and poets gathered here, suggests a more
integrated understanding of who we are, an understanding that depends on
an inner life and an ability to attune to what is. She points toward the soft
eye of looking from within that proceeds through the heart rather than the
piercing eye/ "I" of looking through the mind. To see through one's interiority takes time—but not time alone for without action, effort, even humility and suffering—transformation cannot occur.

In changing position so to tarry yet again with this long ago event, I am
reminded of the importance of slowness, meditative pause, and learning to heed bodily feeling. Indeed, in calling on the third ear, the flesh
of the body, and the soft eye of the heart, this recollection as meander
has unfolded as a kind of synaesthesia. That is, knowing as skin-to-skin,
which "leaves us exposed and without grounds, exposed to the groundless-
ness of the mystery . . . this intractable mystery is the final difficulty that
hermeneutics is bent on restoring" (Caputo, 1987, p. 267). Here, 'without
grounds' does not imply without presence; in fact, it points to the paradox
of a learning-living presence so as to experience mystery—and its 'ground-
lessness' (p. 267).

As Hermes's zigzag demonstrates, hermeneutics strives to keep itself
open to wonder while simultaneously trying to uncover what is hidden.
In other words, as teachers reach through and beyond the biographical to
the archetypal, images, and qualities, even actions previously not seen or
known open, becoming gateways to a more complete existential engagement of their practice. A hermeneutics of trust is inherent to archetypal
reflectivity because something concealed becomes revealed. The Greeks
called this *aletheia*, meaning "the event of concealment and unconcealment" (p. 115). Aletheia works against what is dead—bringing it to life;
"it remembers and unconceals what was forgotten or lost to the business
and 'work of simply getting by'" (Wallace, 1987, 12).

The experience of the lived depth of those island days reveals the world as
"brought in by feeling"—a tactile memory enlivened and known viscerally in
the present (Keller, 1986, p. 183). I am once again with grade ten students and
colleagues from Colegio Bolivar. It is my body as a whole and the whole system of sensorial perception that moves to the invisible experience of bodily
feelings first unconscious, then some pre-conscious, then again some conscious to what is in the world. Yet it is that which moves via the body before

becoming sensate that remains rooted in rich archetypal soil, fundamental, textile and transcendental. In regard to what is seen, Merleau-Ponty (1968) describe it thus:

> the visible about us seems to rest in itself. It is as though our vision were formed in the heart of the visible, or as though there were between it and us an intimacy as between the sea and the strand. (p. 130)

I include Merleau-Ponty here to signal the paradox of seeing and seen, visible and invisible, concealment and unconcealment—that each is necessary for the other while always already in relation. There too is the intermediary, the hyphen, the flesh, as well as the mystery. While Merleau-Ponty privileges sight, its seeing arises through touch and feeling as symbolized by the heart.

For Aristotle, touch is one of the five senses and at the same time the indispensable condition of all the senses. That is, touch brings us into intimate contact with particular physical things while remaining a universal sense that traverses the other four. Most importantly, touch expresses body and soul as a single occasion! Hermeneut Richard Kearney (2015) elaborates:

> Touch is the heart and soul of the senses, the intersensorial link [the "between-two"] and milieu which makes all sensible mediation between the outer and inner world possible in the first place. "Since we touch with our whole body, our soul *is* the act of touch, and only as such can it be a hearing soul, a seeing soul and so on." Touch fosters a synesthetic community of sensing. (Chrétien, 2004 cited in Kearney, 2015, p. 23, emphasis in original)

'Our soul is the act of touch' suggests that we become through "the process of 'feeling' the world, of housing the world in one unit of complex feeling" (Whitehead,1978, p. 80). As Octavio Paz pens,

> I touch you with my eyes
> I watch you with my hands
> I see with my fingertips what my eyes touch. (cited in Kearney, 2015, p. 23)

Running through the imaginal gathering of Poetry, Silence, and the Sea, Hermes appears as a particular kind of Subversive, Elder, and Wise One—a deity behind the scenes, tacking between the archetypes that have enlivened my remembrance and revealed a certain sacredness of the teacher–student relationship. After all, Hermes is God of Silence and Communication; God of Play, Trickery, and Creativity; God of Boundaries, Borders, and the Liminal. While the Sea is the interstitial place to land and sky or to upper and lower worlds, this is Hermes's reign and so his way—hermeneutics—becomes the lived lesson—"a lesson in humility" (Caputo, 1987, p. 258). Too it is a "reflective inquiry concerned with 'our entire understanding of the world and thus . . . all the various forms in which this understanding manifests itself' " (Gadamer cited in Moules et al., 2015, p. 3). While we peer behind language and venture into the contextual world of a word, despite what is said, this process aims at the "unsaid life of our discourses" (Grondin, 1995, p. x).

Gadamer (1989) offered that the venture into the unsaid involves the spec- ulative dimension in language, the mirroring of meanings, and the belief that the said is always in relationship with the unsaid; "we can understand a text only when we've understood the question to which it is an answer" (p. 370). Who and what animates our work—our pedagogic endeavors? In what ways does our teaching reflect our commitments and responsibilities to the world? And if it does not, then what would it take to do so? Living these questions has guided both reflection through and amplification of Silence, Poetry, and the Sea. It too demonstrates the value in always questioning the things that are taken for granted—the disruption of the clear narrative.

Educators, called as Walkaways, Strong Poets, Elders, Pilgrims, and Heroes, bear a responsibility to those in their care: we must critically attend our own psychospiritual development, which includes reparative work through the body, so we are better able to enrich our practice through teacher reflectiv- ity and relationally sensitive teaching methods. In doing so, we contribute to creating and maintaining learning spaces—be they island, classroom, or con- nected urban sites—that are vibrant zones of personal, cultural, and ethical encounter—"sites of pedagogical lifestyle politics" (Mayes, 2007, p. 208).

When we are willing and able to be present, make contact, and listen deeply to our students, our selves, and the Things gathered in learning encounters, we begin to uncover who we/they are. That is, our "real work"— "to make the world as real as it is and to find ourselves as real as we are within it" (Snyder, 1980, p. 82). Philosophically, Robert Bringhurst (2008) speaks similarly of the process of becoming whole. For him, becoming, unfolds through poetry:

> What does poetry say? It says that what-is is: that the real is real, and that it is alive. It speaks the grammar of being. It sings the polyphonic structure of mean- ing itself. . . . Poetry is the language of being: the breath, the voice, the song, the speech of being. It does not need us. We are the ones in need of it. If we haven't learned to hear it, we will also never speak it. (p. 43)

"We are the ones in need of it"—that is, the presence of the realm that "does not need us"—the transpersonal in all its forms and flights. Regardless of the place that has been designated for learning, the setting constellates a field and within it characters, narratival symbols, motifs, and ancestors circulate with great force. At the core of these constellations is the reality that the teacher–student relationship is archetypal. Because the presence of this realm produces a sense of significance, even spiritual meaning in the individual, it is wise to draw upon it in teaching and learning so to animate educational processes.

In the demands of an audit culture, many teachers have turned back to didactic methods, prescribed lessons, and teaching to exams, often unaware of the dangers attached to them. In this turn, they setup and so undergo "misencounters"—a word to designate the failure of a real meeting between teacher and student. It is a "mismeeting" or a traumatic relational experience wherein the fecundity of the lived relationship is lost (Buber cited in Orange, 2010, p. 17). In many ways the "world is not comprehensible but it is embracable through the embracing of one of its beings"—this is a maxim to guide our work (Friedman, 1994, cited in Orange, 2010, p. 31). Perhaps it is even the way in which we must reframe our educational efforts, that is, in "ultimate terms" (Huebner, 1999, p. 405).

If we have spent much of our lives numb and asleep, or in step with the collective, waking up to the individuation process through archetypal reflectivity might be frightening even disconnecting. It is understandable to resist the work. Jung spoke of it in these terms:

> The development of consciousness is the burden, the suffering, and the blessing of kind [human]. Each new discovery leads to greater consciousness, and the path along which we are going is merely an extension of it. This inevitably calls for greater responsibility and enforces a great change in ourselves. We must draw conclusions from what we know and discover, and not take everything for granted. (Jung cited in McGuire & Hull, 1977, p. 248)

Yet, just as the experiences of such a long ago field trip opened up relationships, dynamics, learning, dreaming, and our bodies, we lost our edges, and so found each other—if only briefly. Bodies and souls lost their borders to each other, where at times we became both immaterial spirit and physical reality, a "meaningful system of body living within the flesh" (Hillman, 1967, p. 121).

It is the promise of such a fleeting meeting that has drawn many of us to the art and craft of teaching, that is, to explore an issue or subject that we love, with students whom we wish to nurture, in ways that are deeply meaningful to teachers and students (us) at all levels of their (our) being. As Cliff Mayes (2007) has so beautifully written: "Teaching from their depths to their students' depths allows teachers to find deeper satisfaction in their vital work as they foster psychodynamic and ethical growth in their students" (p. 210). It is our hope that our book will be of service to teachers in their pedagogic endeavors.

To close this section, a final gesture from Neruda:

> I have to learn
> to swim inside my dreams
> in case the sea should come
> and visit me in my sleep.
> And if that happens, all will be well,
> and when tomorrow stirs
> on the wet stones, the sand
> and the great resounding sway of sea
> will know who I am and why I return,
> will accept me into their school.
>
> And I can be content again
> in the solitude of the sand,
> graduated by the wind
> and respected by the sea-world. (Neruda, 2003c, p. 31)

NOTES

1 Because body and presence are critical concepts and processes to learning (and so this chapter), it is important to flag Jack Rosenberg's (1987) concept "Blue Light" and its analogous nature to the quality of relationship to which I felt unconsciously called and in response have come to embody in my pedagogic and psychotherapeutic practices. According to body psychotherapy and attachment theory, the energetic quality of "mother"/caregiver makes for successful bonding, rather than her/his/their mere physical presence (which might be fragmented, distracted, traumatized, disembodied). Proper reflection or authentic mirroring of the child in energetic terms has been described, "by likening the mother's quality to a 'Blue Light'" (p. 151). If she/he/they had adequate bonding and proper reflection as children, they received "Blue Light" and can pass it along to their children—and I would add to others with whom one is in close, caring relationship. Blue Light is compounded by warmth, love, trust, respect, acceptance, and humour. Children raised in a Blue Light feel generally good about themselves. If a child does not experience accurate mirroring, she/he/they lose touch—contact/relation—with the fragile developing Self. "The loss of this connection leads to fragmentation or loss of identity accompanied by a total mind/body/emotional experience of annihilation" (p. 151).

2 The intentional inclusion of multiple personal pronouns seeks to respect diverse identifications, especially those who stand on the continuum, between and beyond, the hegemonic markers of "male" and "female"—typically referred to with the personal pronouns: he/him/his and she/her/hers. Among some genderqueer, non-binary, gender creative, questioning, trans, and Two-Spirit people, "they/them" (or most accurately they/them/their/theirs) is/has become a choice of personal pronoun (along with *ze/zir* and others). In solidarity with, respect for, and inclusivity

of friends, colleagues, and diverse readership, "they" will be used alone as well as alongside "she" and or "he." When herein used, note the Standard English language rule of pronoun-noun agreement will not be followed. In support of the campaign to raise awareness of gender neutral pronouns and diversity in gender identities, see: https://www.su.ualberta.ca/services/thelanding/learn/pronouns/. I would like to thank Alison Brooks-Starks who shared this site with me and offered comment on this footnote.

3   Published works that have explored teacher archetypal reflectivity have to date called upon Greek gods and goddesses and images of human forms such as Clown, Trickster, Great Mother/Father, Queen/King, Lover, and Warrior. While these forms are certainly beneficial, I urge educators to reflect upon their own cultural influences (for example, Celtic, Zulu, Cree), and not only "human forms" but also of concepts or processes (such as Poetry/Poetic and Silence). As this is a relatively new arena for teacher education and teacher professional development, the possibilities for amplification are numerous.

4   "Emptiness" here as in Buddhist thought means the true nature of things and encounters. As the Dalai Lama explains in his writing on the Heart Sutra, "all phenomena in their own-being are empty." "Own-being" means separate independent existence. The passage underscores the interconnected nature of all things, our co-rising interdependence. That is, everything is a tentative expression of one seamless, fluxing landscape. No thing (be it person, text, mountain) possesses any permanent, fixed identity.

5   Teachers called by these archetypal images can learn much from Hermes who had to bridge an ontological gap, a gap between the thinking of the gods and that of humans—as in education between the thinking of theorists, policy makers, even administrators and that of youth. Hermes:

> bridged the difference between the visible and the invisible, and between dreams and waking, between the unconscious and the conscious. He is the quicksilver god ["Mercury" in Latin] of sudden insights, ideas, inspirations. And he is also the trickster god of thefts, highway robbery and of sudden windfalls of good luck. . . . He is god of crossroads and boundaries; . . . [and] as psychopomp, he led the dead to the underworld, so he 'crossed the line' between the living and the dead, between the living human world and the underworld of Hades. Hermes is truly the 'god of the gaps,' of the margins, the boundaries, the limins of many things. (Brown cited in Orange, 2010, p. 2; see Fidyk, 2010 for additional description)

6   In order to have empathy for another, one requires the capacity and ability to be present and attuned. If students and teachers struggle to remain embodied, perhaps even lack the awareness of what this looks like and how to do it, then being empathetic toward another will be limited at best.

7   In the individual-group dynamic of scapegoating there are three kinds of participants: The scapegoat, the scapegoaters, and the walkaways. Walkaways are the subgroup blessed and cursed by the weight of sensitivity and an empathetic nature to the plight of the scapegoat. They are called to carry the scapegoat complex. Some walkaways identify wit the scapegoat and leave the group because they do not yet have enough ego strength to take up the hero's task; others take on the task of

scapegoat hero but are overcome by its energy. The third way of the walkaway is sha-man, healer, or teacher—the way of the conscious scapegoat. They locate themselves on the margins of society—partially in and partially out. The walkaway's stance is both a way of being and a way of knowing. The walkaway must come to relate con-sciously to the meaning of the scapegoat, only then might healing occur. This stance is a commitment and an attitude not a prescription (Fidyk, 2013b).

8   This marker is a tricky one. It is valuable when using this analogy to include Salvio's argument that the "position of the good enough mother requires women to overwrite their own desires with those of their children, and to deny the rage, pain, fear, and ambivalence that is an inevitable part of mothering" (2006, p. 67). The scholarship of M. Grumet (1988) elaborates further on the ways that the ideals of motherhood have affected educators' notions of what it means to be a good teacher, and how such goodness is assessed.

9   While I use "erotic" here to designate any activity where the body is involved, Jung too did not make a sharp linguistic split between the spiritual and the erotic. For him, these are "both aspects of the same 'numinosity' of the psyche, irreducible to either" (Kailo, 1997, p. 190). In psychotherapy, we articulate the psychic "unsaid" as what ever dreams and waking fantasies seek to express—and Jung referred to "shadow," the contrasexual "anima" and "animus," and the perspective of the Self as "the total-psyche-in-potentia" (cited in Kailo, 1997, p. 191).

REFERENCES

Ackerman, D. (1999). *Deep play*. New York, NY: Vintage Books.

Aoki, T. (1986/1991/2005). Teaching as indwelling between two curriculum worlds. In W. Pinar & R. Irwin (Eds.), *Curriculum in a new key: The collected works of Ted T. Aoki* (pp. 159–165). Mahwah, NJ: Lawrence Erlbaum Associates Inc.

Ayto, J. (1993). *Dictionary of word origins: The histories of more than 8,000 English-language words*. New York, NY: Arcade Publishing.

Bateson, M. C. (1994). *Peripheral visions: Learning along the way*. New York, NY: HarperCollins.

Bold, G. M., & Salvio, P. M. (2006). *Love's return: Psychoanalytic essays on child-hood, teaching, and learning*. New York, NY: Routledge.

Bringhurst, R. (2007). Everywhere being is dancing, knowing is known. In R. Brin-ghurst (Ed.), *Everywhere being is dancing: Twenty pieces of thinking* (pp. 15–16). Kentville, NS: Gaspereau Press.

Bringhurst, R. (2008). *The tree of meaning: Language, mind and ecology*. Berkeley, CA: Counterpoint.

Britzman, D. (1998). *Lost objects, contested objects: Toward a psychoanalytic inquiry of learning*. Albany, NY: State University of New York Press.

Britzman, D. (2003). *After-education: Anna Freud, Melanie Klein, and psychoana-lytic histories of learning*. Albany, NY: State University of New York Press.

Britzman, D. (2006). *Novel education: Psychoanalytic studies of learning and not learning*. Albany, NY: State University of New York Press.

Britzman, D. (2009). *The very thought of education: Psychoanalysis and the impossible professions*. Albany, NY: State University of New York Press.

Britzman, D. (2015). *A psychoanalyst in the classroom: On the human condition in education*. Albany, NY: State University of New York Press.

Buber, M. (1958). *I and Thou. Second edition with a postscript by the author*. Trans. R. G. Smith. Edinburgh: T & T Clark.

Buber, M. (1988). *The knowledge of man: Selected essays*. Atlantic Highlands, NJ: Humanities Press International.

Buber, M. (1999). *Martin Buber on psychology and psychotherapy: Essays, letters, and dialogue* (J. Buber Agassi, Ed.). New York, NY: Syracuse University Press.

Buhner, S. H. (2004). *The secret teachings of plants: The intelligence of the heart in the direct perception of nature*. Rochester, VT: Bear & Co.

Caputo, J. (1987). *Radical hermeneutics*. Bloomington, IN: Indiana University Press.

Caranfa, S. (2014). Silence as the foundation of learning. *Educational Theory, 54*(2), 211–231.

Cheetham, T. (2003). *The world turned inside out: Henry Corbin and Islamic mysticism*. Woodstock, CT: Spring Journal Books.

Cirlot, J. E. (2014). *A dictionary of symbols*. New York, NY: Welcome Rain Publishers.

Dauenhauer, B. (1980). *Silence: The phenomenon and its ontological significance*. Bloomington, IN: Indiana University Press.

derby, m. w. (2015). *Place, being, resonance: A critical ecohermeneutic approach to education*. New York, NY: Peter Lang.

Dobson, D. (2008a). *Transformative teaching: Promoting transformation through literature, the arts, and Jungian psychology*. Rotterdam, The Netherlands: Sense Publishers.

Dobson, D. (2008b). The symbol as teacher: Reflective practices and methodology in transformative education. In R. A. Jones, A. Clarkson, S. Congram, & N. Stratton (Eds.), *Education & imagination: Post-Jungian perspectives* (pp. 142–159). Hove: Routledge.

Dobson, D. (2009). Royal, Warrior, Magician, Lover: Archetypal reflectivity and the construction of professional knowledge. *Teacher Education Quarterly, 36*(3), 149–165.

Doll, M. (2000). *Like letters in running water: A mythopoetics of curriculum*. Mahwah, NJ: Lawrence Erlbaum.

Doll, M. (2011). *The more of myth: A pedagogy of diversion*. Rotterdam, The Netherlands: Sense Publishers.

Doll, M. (2017). *The mythopoetics of currere: Memories, dreams, and literary texts as teaching avenues to self-study*. New York: Routledge.

Domanski, D. (2002). The wisdom of falling. Don Domanski interviewed by S. D. Johnson. In T. Bowling (Ed.), *Where the words come from: Canadian poets in conversation* (pp. 244–255). Roberts Creek, BC: Nightwood Editions.

Domanski, D. (2006). *Poetry and the sacred*. Nanaimo, BC: Institute for Coastal Research.

Equilibrium. (n.d.). Retrieved from https://www.etymonline.com/search?q=equilibrium

Farinella, E. (1976). Michele Federico Sciacca. *Studies: An Irish Quarterly Review, 65*(258), 144–150.

Farley, L. (2014). Drawing trauma: The therapeutic potential of witnessing the child's visual testimony of War. *Journal of the American Psychoanalytic Association, 62*(5), 835–854.

Felman, S. (1987). *Jacques Lacan and the adventure of insight: Psychoanalysis in contemporary culture*. Cambridge, MA: Harvard University Press.

Felman, S. (1992). *Testimony: Crisis of witnessing, psychoanalysis, and history*. New York: Routledge.

Fidyk, A. (2008). Writing and speaking silence. In B. Warland (Ed.), *Silence in teaching and learning* (p. 30). Ottawa: Council of 3M National Teaching Fellows & Society for Teaching and Learning in Higher Education.

Fidyk, A. (2009). A "rehabilitation of eros": Cultivating a conscious relation with love [invited article]. *Jung Journal: Culture & Psyche, 3*(4), 59–68. Retrieved from http://www.tandfonline.com/doi/abs/10.1525/jung.2009.3.4.59#.VQyTaEJhcmY

Fidyk, A. (2010). Hermaphrodite as healing image: Connecting a mythic imagination to education. *Jungian Journal of Scholarly Studies, 6*(2). Retrieved from http://jungiansociety.org/images/e-journal/Volume-6/Fidyk-2010.pdf

Fidyk, A. (2013a). Attuned to silence: A pedagogy of presence. In S. Malhotra & A. Carrillo Rowe (Eds.), *Silence and power: Feminist reflections on the edges of sound* (pp. 114–128). New York, NY: Palgrave Macmillan.

Fidyk, A. (2013b). Buddha as a walkaway [invited]. *Spring: A Journal of Archetype and Culture. Buddhism and Depth Psychology: Refining the Encounter, 89*, pp. 90–101. New Orleans, LA: Spring Journal.

Fidyk, A. (2014). "Intruders," "animal roots" and "Mother Earth": Tracking the art complex in the work of Emily Carr. *International Journal of Jungian Studies, 6*(1), 3–22.

Fidyk, A. (2016a). Unconscious ties that bind: Attending to complexes in the classroom, Part 1. *International Journal of Jungian Studies, 8*(3), 181–194.

Fidyk, A. (2016b). Unconscious ties that bind: Attending to complexes in the classroom, Part 2. *International Journal of Jungian Studies, 8*(3), 195–210.

Fidyk, A. (2017). A setting of things side by side. In P. Sameshima, A. Fidyk, J. Kedrick, & C. Leggo (Eds.), *Poetic inquiry: Enchantment of place* (pp. 32–37). Wilmington, DE: Vernon Press.

Finke, L. (1997). Knowledge as bait: Feminism, voice, and the pedagogical unconscious. In S. Todd (Ed.), *Learning desire: Perspectives on pedagogy, culture, and the unsaid* (pp. 117–139). New York, NY: Routledge.

Fiumara, G. C. (1990). *The other side of language: A philosophy of listening*. London: Hobbs.

Freire, A. M. A. (Ed). (2007). *Daring to dream: Toward a pedagogy of the unfinished*. Boulder, CO: Paradigm Publishers.

Freire, P. (1998). *Pedagogy of freedom: Ethics, democracy, and civic courage.* Oxford: Rowman & Littlefield Publishers.

Gadamer, H.-G. (1989). Truth and Method (2nd ed.) New York: Crossroad.

Gadamer, H.-G. (1991). *Truth and method.* Trans. J. Weinsheimer & D. Marshall, 2nd ed. New York, NY: Crossroads. (Original work published 1960)

Gadamer, H.-G. & Hahn, L. E. (1997). *The philosophy of Hans-Georg Gadamer.* Chicago, IL: Open Court.

Glenn, C. (2004). *Unspoken: A rhetoric of silence.* Carbondale, IL: Southern Illinois University Press.

Greene, M. (1995). *Releasing the imagination: Essays on education, the arts, and social change.* San Francisco, CA: Jossey-Bass.

Greene, M. (2005). Countering indifference: The role of the arts. *Newsletter of the California Council on Teacher Education, 15*(2), 1–19. Retrieved from http://ccte.org/wp-content/pdfs-newsletters/ccte-news-2005-summer.pdf

Greene, M. (2007). *Imagination and becoming* (Bronx charter school of the arts). Retrieved from http://www.maxinegreene.org/articles.php

Grondin, J. (1995). *Sources of hermeneutics.* Albany, NY: SUNY Press.

Grumet, M. (1988). *Bitter milk: Women and teaching.* Amherst, MA: University of Massachusetts Press.

Guggenbühl-Craig, A. (1971). *Power in the helping professions.* Dallas, TX: Spring.

Gustafson, R. (1987). *Plummets and other partialities.* Victoria, BC: Sono Nis Press.

Hillman, J. (1967). *Insearch: Psychology and religion.* New York, NY: Scribners.

Hirshfield, J. (1997). *Nine gates: Entering the mind of poetry.* New York, NY: Harper Perennial.

Holmes, J. (2001). *The search for the secure base: Attachment theory and psycho-therapy.* East Sussex, UK: Brunner-Routledge.

Huebner, D. (1999). *The lure of the transcendent: Collected essays by Dwayne E. Huebner.* V. Hillis (Ed.). London: Lawrence Erlbaum Associates.

Intuition. n.d. Retrieved from https://www.etymonline.com/word/intuition

Irigaray, L. (1991). The limits of the transference. In M. Whitford (Ed.), *The Irigaray reader* (p. 113). Oxford: Basil Blackwell.

Jung, C. G. (1921/1990). Psychological types. *The collected works of C. G. Jung* (R. F. C. Hull, Trans.). Volume 6. Princeton, NJ: Princeton University Press.

Jung, C. G. (1930/1978). Psychology and literature. In *The spirit in man, art, and literature, The collected works of C. G. Jung.* (Trans R. F. C. Hull; pp. 84–105). In H. Read, M. Fordham, G. Adler, & W. McGuire (Eds.), Bollingen Series 15. Princeton, NJ: Princeton University Press.

Jung, C. G. (1963/1989). *Mysterium coniunctionis: An inquiry into the separation and synthesis of psychic opposites in alchemy* (Trans. R. F. C. Hull). In H. Read, M. Fordham, G. Adler, & W. McGuire (Eds.), Bollingen Series 14. Princeton, NJ: Princeton University Press.

Kaepernick. C. (2017, September 7). The awakening of Colin Kaepernick. *New York Times.* Retrieved https://www.nytimes.com/2017/09/07/sports/colin-kaepernick-nfl-protests.html

Karen, R. (1994). *Becoming attached: Unfolding the mystery of the infant-mother bond and its impact on later life*. New York, NY: Warner Books.

Kearney, R. (2015). The wager of carnal hermeneutics. In R. Kearney & B. Treanor (Eds.), *Carnal hermeneutics* (pp. 15–56). New York, NY: Fordham University Press.

Keller, C. (1986). *From a broken web: Separation, sexism, and self*. Boston: Beacon Press.

Lane, J. (2006). *The spirit of silence: Making space for creativity*. White River Junction, VT: Chelsea Green Publishing.

Lee, D. (1998). *Body music*. Toronto, ON: Anansi Press.

Lees, H. E. (2012). *Silence in schools*. London: Institute of Education Press.

Lilburn, T. (1999). "How to be here." In *Living in the world as if it were home: Essays* (p. 6). Dunvegan, ON: Cormorant Books.

Lilburn, T. (2002). *Thinking and singing: Poetry and the practice of philosophy*. Toronto, ON: Cormorant.

Lindley, D. A. (1993). *This rough magic: The life of teaching*. Westport, CT: Bergin & Garvey.

Lindley, D. A. (2006). *On life's journey: Always becoming*. Wilmette, IL: Chiron Publications.

Marion, J.-L. (2007). *The erotic phenomenon*. Trans. S. E. Lewis. Chicago, IL: Chicago University Press.

Martin, K. (Ed.) (2010). *The book of symbols: Reflections on archetypal images*. Los Angeles, CA: Taschen.

Mayes, C. (2005). *Jung and education: Elements of an archetypal pedagogy*. Lanham, MD: Rowman & Littlefield Education.

Mayes, C. (2010). *The archetypal Hero's journey in teaching and learning: A study in Jungian pedagogy*. Madison, WI: Atwood Publishing.

McGuire, W., & Hull, R. F. C. (Eds.). (1977). *C. G. Jung speaking: Interviews and encounters*. Princeton, NJ: Princeton University Press.

McKay, D. (1995). Thoughts on ravens, home, and nature poetry. In T. Lilburn (Ed.), *Poetry and knowing: Speculative essays and interviews* (pp. 17–22). Kingston, ON: Quarry Press.

McKay, D. (2002). The bushtits' nest. In Tim Lilburn (Ed.), *Thinking and singing: Poetry and the practice of philosophy*. Toronto, ON: Cormorant.

Merker, H. (2000). *Listening: Ways of hearing in a silent world*. Dallas, TX: Southern Methodist University Press.

Merleau-Ponty, M. (1968). *The visible and the invisible*. Evanston, IL: Northwestern University Press.

Merskin, D. (2007). Flagging patriotism: The myth of Old Glory. *Jung Journal: Culture & Psyche, 1*(4), 11–16.

Michelfelder, D. P., & Palmer, R. E. (1989). *Dialogue and deconstruction: The Gadamer-Derrida encounter*. Albany, NY: State University of New York Press.

Moore, R., & Gillette, D. (1990). *King, warrior, magician, lover: Rediscovering the archetypes of the mature masculine*. New York, NY: HarperCollins.

Moules, N., McCaffrey, G., Field, J., & Laing, C. (2015). *Conducting hermeneutic research: From philosophy to practice*. New York, NY: Peter Lang.

Muller, R. T. (2015). *Trauma and the avoidant client: Attachment-based strategies for healing*. New York: W. W. Norton & Co.

Nader, K. O. (2006). Childhood trauma: The deeper wound. In J. P. Wilson (Ed.), *The posttraumatic self: Restoring meaning and wholeness to personality*. New York, NY: Routledge.

Neilsen, L. (1998). *Knowing her place: Research literacies and feminist occasions*. San Francisco, CA; Big Tancook Island, NS: Caddo Gap Press & Backalong Books.

Neruda, P. (1968/2008). "Close to the knives." In *The hands of day* (pp. 53–57). (Trans. W. O'Daly). Port Townsend, WA: Copper Canyon Press.

Neruda, P. (1969). "Poetry." In *Love: Ten poems by Pablo Neruda* (pp. 7–9). (Trans. W. S. Merwin). New York, NY: Hyperion. (Originally published in 1924)

Neruda, P. (1971/1984). "XXII." In *Pablo Neruda: Still another day* (p. 57). (Trans. W. O'Daly). Port Townsend, WA: Copper Canyon Press.

Neruda, P. (1977). *Memoirs*. (Trans. H. St. Martin). New York, NY: Farrar, Straus, Giroux.

Neruda, P. (1984). *Passions and impressions*. (Trans. M. Sayes Peden). M. Neruda & M. Otero Silva (Eds.). New York, NY: Farrar, Straus, Giroux.

Neruda, P. (2002a). "Time that wasn't lost." In *The yellow heart* (p. 69). (Trans. W. O'Daly). Port Townsend, WA: Copper Canyon Press.

Neruda, P. (2002b). "Is the sea there?" In *Pablo Neruda: The sea and the bells* (p. 111). (Trans. W. O'Daly). Port Townsend, WA: Copper Canyon Press.

Neruda, P. (2003a). "The sea." In *On the blue shore of silence: Poems of the sea* (p. 3). (Trans. A. Reid). New York, NY: HarperCollins.

Neruda, P. (2003b). "Here, there, everywhere." In *On the blue shore of silence: Poems of the sea* (p. 25). (Trans. A. Reid). New York, NY: HarperCollins.

Neruda, P. (2003c). "Strangers on the shore." In *On the blue shore of silence: Poems of the sea* (pp. 29–31). (Trans. A. Reid). New York, NY: HarperCollins.

Neruda, P. (n.d.a). "The wide ocean." Retrieved from https://www.poemhunter.com/poem/the-wide-ocean/

Neruda, P. (n.d.b). "XXXIV (You are the daughter of the sea)." Retrieved from https://hellopoetry.com/poem/9961/xxxiv-you-are-the-daughter-of-the-sea/

Neruda, P. (n.d.c). "I would like for you to be still." Retrieved from https://hellopoetry.com/poem/9922/i-like-for-you-to-be-still/

Neville, B. (2012). *The life of things: Therapy and the soul of the world*. Herefordshire, UK: PCCS Books.

Ng-A-Fook, N., Ibrahim, A., & Reis, G. (Eds.) (2016). *Provoking curriculum studies: Strong poetry and arts of the possible in education*. New York, NY: Routledge.

Oliveros, P. (2005). *Deep listening: A composer's sound practice*. New York, NY: iUniverse, Inc.

Orange, D. M. (1995). *Emotional understanding: Studies in psychoanalytic epistemology*. New York, NY: Guilford Press.

Orange, D. M. (2010). *Thinking for clinicians: Philosophical resources for contemporary psychoanalysis and the humanistic psychotherapies.* New York, NY: Routledge.

O'Reilley, M. R. (1998). *Radical presence: Teaching as contemplative practice.* Portsmouth, NH: Boynton/Cook Publishers.

Packer, T. (2007). *The silent question: Meditating in the stillness of not-knowing.* Boston, MA: Shambhala.

Picard, M. (1948/2002). *The world of silence.* Wichita, KS: Eighth Day Press.

Pitt, A. (2003). *The play of the personal: Psychoanalytic narratives of feminist education.* New York, NY: Peter Lang.

Pitt, A., & Britzman, D. (2003). Speculations on qualities of difficult knowledge in teaching and learning: An experiment in psychoanalytic research. *International Journal of Qualitative Studies in Education, 16*(6), 755–776.

Poirot, L. (1990). *Pablo Neruda: Absence and Presence.* (Trans. A. Reid). New York, NY: W. W. Norton & Co.

Prendergast, M. (2009). Introduction. In M. Prendergast, C. Leggo, & P. Sameshima (Eds.), *Poetic inquiry: Vibrant voices in the social sciences* (pp. xix–xli). Rotterdam: The Netherlands Sense Pub.

Rautins, C., & Ibrahim, A. (2011). Wide-awakeness: Toward a critical pedagogy of imagination, humanism, agency, and becoming. *International Journal of Critical Pedagogy, 3*(3), 24–36.

Rich, A. (2001). *Arts of the possible: Essays & conversations.* New York, NY: W. W. Norton & Co.

Robertson, D. L. (1996). Facilitating transformative learning: Attending to the dynamics of the educational helping relationship. *Adult Education Quarterly, 47*(1) 41–53.

Rorty, R. (1989). *Contingency, irony, and solidarity.* Cambridge, UK: Cambridge University Press.

Schilpp, P. A., Friedman, M. S., & Buber, M. (1967). *The philosophy of Martin Buber.* La Salle, IL: Open Court.

Sheldrake, R. (1995/2012). *Presence of the past.* Rochester, VT: Park Street Press.

Smith, D. (1999). *Pedagon: Interdisciplinary essays in the human sciences, pedagogy and culture.* New York, NY: Peter Lang.

Smith, D. (2014). *Teaching as the practice of wisdom.* New York, NY: Bloomsbury Academic.

Snyder, G. (1980). *The real work: Interviews and talks, 1964–1979 by Gary Snyder.* Cambridge, MA: New Directions.

Stein, M. (2006a). *Principle of individuation: Toward the development of human consciousness.* Wilmette, IL: Chiron Publications.

Stein, M. (2006b). On the importance of numinous experience in the alchemy of individuation. In A. Casement & D. Tracey (Eds.), *The idea of the numinous* (pp. 34–52). London: Routhedge.

Stern, J. (2012). *Loneliness and solitude in education: How to value individuality and create an enstatic school.* Frankfurt am Main, Germany: Peter Lang.

Stromsted, T., & Sieff, D. (2015). Dances of psyche and soma: Re-inhabiting the body in the wake of emotional trauma. *Understanding and healing emotional trauma: Conversations with pioneering clinicians and researchers* (pp. 46–63). New York, NY: Routledge.

Taubman, P. M. (2012). *Disavowed knowledge: Psychoanalysis, education, and teaching.* New York, NY: Routledge.

Teaching wide-awake. (2008, October 14). Retrieved from https://teachingwide-awake.wordpress.com/2008/10/14/wide-awakeness/

Todd, S. (1997a). Looking at pedagogy in 3-D: Rethinking difference, disparity, and desire. In S. Todd (Ed.), *Learning desire: Perspectives on pedagogy, culture, and the unsaid* (pp. 237–260). New York, NY: Routledge.

Todd, S. (1997b). *Learning from the other: Levinas, psychoanalysis, and ethical possibilities in education.* Albany, NY: State University of New York Press.

Van den Berk, T. (2012). *Jung and art: The autonomy of the creative drive.* Hove: Routledge.

Van der Kolk, B. (2014). *The body keeps the score: Brain, mind, and body in the healing of trauma.* New York, NY: Penguin Books.

Wakefield, C. (2016). *In search of Aphrodite: Women, archetypes and sex therapy.* New York, NY: Routledge.

Wallace, B. (1987). The stubborn particulars of grace. Toronto, ON: McClelland & Stewart.

Weil, S. (1952). *Gravity and grace.* Lincoln, NE: University of Nebraska Press.

Whitehead, A. N. (1929/1967). *The aims of education and other essays.* New York, NY: Free Press.

Whitehead, A. N. (1978). *Process and Reality: An Essay in Cosmology.* D.R. Griffin & D.W. Sherburne (Eds.). New York: Free Press.

Winnicott, D. W. (1971/2005). *Playing and reality.* London: Routledge.

Wolff, T. (1951). *Structural forms of the feminine psyche.* (Trans. P. Watzlawik). Zurich: C. G. Jung Institute.

Wyatt, S. (2017). Medial women: Views of a feminist epistemologist. In L. Gardner & F. Gray (Eds.), *Feminist views from somewhere: Post-Jungian themes in feminist theory.* New York, NY: Routledge.

Zembylas, M., & Michaelides, P. (2004). The sound of silence in pedagogy. *Educational Theory, 54*(2), 193–210.

Zwicky, J. (1992). *Lyric philosophy.* Toronto, ON: University of Toronto Press.

Zwicky, J. (2003). *Wisdom & metaphor.* Kentville, NS: Gaspereau Press.

Zwicky, J. (2008). Lyric realism: Nature poetry, silence and ontology. *The Malahat Review, 165* (Winter), 85–91.

Zwicky, J. (2012). *Auden as philosopher: How poets think* (The Ralph Gustafson Lecture Vancouver Island University, October 20, 2011). Nanaimo, BC: Institute for Coastal Research.

Conclusion

Reclaiming the Fire

In this book, we have tried to assist you, the teacher, as you explore and expand your sense of calling in your work, which is second to none in its psychological, social, and ethical importance. We feel that being supportive of teachers—who by and large not only do *competent* work but *excellent* work, and carry it on with a heroic dedication to their students—is particularly important now, for criticism of teachers grows louder and louder in the United States. In one sense, this problem is not new.

Since the foundations of public schools were set in the United States about 140 years ago, they have been threatened by individuals, political movements, and governmental agencies and edicts that have aimed at standardizing education and rendering the teacher merely a functionary to implement one-size-fits-all, ready-made agendas, usually of a corporate nature. Teachers have almost always resisted, sometimes successfully, sometimes not (Cremin, 1988). Still, it is true that never in the history of U.S. public education have teachers been required to teach an overly determined curriculum that is geared against a uniform test as they are today.

Naturally, the anonymity and uniformity of standardization threaten teachers' sense of calling. That calling is rooted in teachers' love of children, their passion for their subject matter, and their conviction that they are nobly carrying on a civic mission, which they justifiably feel uniquely qualified to carry out. Understandably, they prize a high degree of freedom in how they go about their craft. Our hope is that by supporting teachers in all of this, they can, through self-renewal, find ways not only to resist the external forces that are trying to objectify them but also to grow internally as teachers in ways that enrich their larger life narrative.

Our discussion of self-object theorists was designed to provide you from a psychoanalytic perspective what you already know from experiential and

135

intuitive perspectives—namely, that it is in loving and lively interaction in the classroom that true learning occurs. Such interaction is precisely what standardized education works to erase because it is too "messy" and completely unmeasurable. We honor you as teachers for keeping such interaction alive in your classrooms as you strive to aid in your students' healthy ego-formation, especially their *learning-ego* formation.

At the same time, however, we have stressed that the teacher should not put too heavy a burden on herself in attaining this goal. Teachers, like most people in the helping professions, take on their vocation out of the moral and emotional impulse to be of service to others. They often have thin boundaries, overextend themselves, and sometimes get unhealthily enmeshed with the client, patient, or student.

That is why it is important that you should always bear in mind that it is the *good-enough teacher* who best helps the student grow in a *good-enough classroom* which, free of perfectionism but infused with an organic ethos of responsibility, allows for creativity. Paradoxically but indisputably, the good-enough teacher is a better teacher than the one who wears herself and her students out with a crazy-making demand for perfection.

From a philosophical vantage point, we have suggested other grounds for your principled resistance and holistic growth as teachers by exploring key concepts in the works of Existentialist theologians Martin Buber and Paul Tillich.

Buber's insistence that goodness resides in mutually nourishing I-Thou relationships is a morally powerful rejoinder to the sterile rhetoric of standardization, whose agenda is to objectify teachers and students—Buber called them I-It nonrelationships. Tillich's idea of "ultimacy" provides sound philosophical scaffolding to the teacher's and student's fundamental need to study those things that are most central to their existence—what are called their "fiduciary commitments" in the language of formal ethics. This does not mean that practical things are unimportant or that facts need not be learned. But it does mean that when education is reduced to students merely memorizing facts and the contents of state-approved curricula in order to regurgitate them on tests, it is catastrophic not only emotionally but also ethically.

In our lengthy analysis of Jungian psychology and its educational uses, we wished to help you reflect in the deepest possible psychospiritual terms on the archetypal significance of your calling as teachers. From Jung, we learned that putting the transcendent self at the center of psychological functioning and forging ties between it and ego-based consciousness is key to finding durable health, cultivating creative potential, and establishing a link between the everyday world and higher vision. We are confident that in engaging in archetypal reflectivity you will find renewed purpose and redoubled strength in this invigorating understanding of your work in its most ancient depths and most timeless heights.

We honor you and will be highly gratified if this book is of service to you in resisting those *outer* forces that threaten the integrity of education. We will be similarly gratified if we have helped you recognize and continue to build upon the ancient, transcendent *inner* power that you, as a teacher, uniquely possess.

We will be gratified if we have given you some theories and terms that will help you in making your case for more humane schooling. The power of a teacher is great. The power of organized teachers is even greater. But the power of teachers united in grand ideas and language is greatest of all. This book was written to aid you in uniting and speaking out of high philosophical purpose and in compelling philosophical language.

Appendix A: Typology and Stress

ESTJ—THE SUPERVISOR

What stresses out an ESTJ:

- Being in an environment that is in disarray
- Frequent disruptions
- Irrational behavior
- Being surrounded by (or guilty of) incompetence
- Unexpected changes
- Lack of control
- Laziness in others
- Not having their strongly held values validated
- Guilt over being critical toward others
- Dealing too long with abstract or theoretical concepts
- Being in a highly charged emotional environment for too long

When overwhelmed by stress, ESTJs often feel isolated from others. They feel as if they are misunderstood and undervalued, and that their efforts are taken for granted. When under stress, they have a hard time putting their feelings into words and communicating them to others. If they are under frequent, chronic stress, they may fall into the grip of their inferior function and introverted feeling. When this happens, they can develop a "martyr complex." The ESTJ will be uncharacteristically emotional; withdraw from others; become hypersensitive about their relationships; and misinterpret tiny, insignificant details into personal attacks. Physically, they may feel tension headaches, and neck or shoulder aches from tension in their body.

How to help an ESTJ experiencing stress:

- Give them some time to be left alone during and immediately after an incident.
- Avoid directly attacking the problem right away.
- Help them break down larger projects into smaller pieces.
- Listen to them. Let them talk it out.
- After some time of listening, discuss information or ideas that could lead to solutions.
- Validate their feelings.
- Don't be overly sympathetic.
- Don't respond emotionally.

ISTJ—THE INSPECTOR

What stresses out an ISTJ:

- Being in an environment that is in disarray
- Looming deadlines
- Being forced or asked to do things that don't make sense to them
- Being asked to do something without a plan or direction
- Frequent change
- Having to innovate without any past experience to rely on
- Being asked to do something spontaneously
- Too much extraversion (excess people contact)
- Emotionally charged situations
- Unfamiliar surroundings
- Dealing too long with abstract or theoretical concepts

When faced with stress overload, ISTJs may fall into "catastrophe mode," where they see nothing but all the potential of what could go wrong. They may beat themselves up, berating themselves for things that could have been done differently or duties that they failed to perform. They will lose their ability to see things calmly and reasonably, and can become depressed at what they see as a bleak future. Under chronic stress, the ISTJ may fall into the grip of their inferior function and extroverted intuition, and become a "dramatizer." They may become intensely angry, rigid in what they're doing, outwardly critical, pessimistic, and embrace an overwhelming fear of the future.

How to help an ISTJ experiencing stress:

- Give them plenty of space.
- Listen and provide provable affirmation of how they've overcome or done something well in the past.
- Break a task down into manageable pieces.
- Do not give generalized compliments.
- Put things that have to be done in sequential order.
- Don't brainstorm. If they are in the grip of their inferior function, extroverted intuition, brainstorming will only make things worse.
- Don't give them more to do. Give them a break from responsibilities if possible.
- Take them seriously. Don't patronize or judge them.
- Encourage them to exercise (without sounding insulting).

ISFJ—THE PROTECTOR

What stresses out an ISFJ:

- Overexerting themselves by saying "yes" to too many projects.
- Conflict or criticism
- Lack of positive feedback
- Environments filled with tension
- Looming deadlines
- Being asked to do things in a way that isn't clearly defined
- Having to overuse their type by having to constantly act as "the responsible one"
- Dealing too long with abstract or theoretical concepts.
- Unfamiliar territory or an uncertain future

When faced with stress, ISFJs become discouraged and depressed. They start to imagine all the things that could go wrong, and they may feel a strong sense of inadequacy. They may feel that everything is all wrong, or that they can't do anything right. If they are in a state of chronic stress, they may fall into the grip of their inferior function, extraverted intuition. When this happens they may start acting completely out of character. They may be at odds with normally relied upon facts and details, they may see everything as awful and feel "doomed." They may become withdrawn, angry, irritable, and pessimistic. They will probably feel emotionally overwhelmed and find themselves worrying about all kinds of horrible possibilities.

How to help an ISFJ experiencing stress:

• Give them space or time alone to work through their feelings.
• Provide provable affirmations about ways they've overcome situations like this in the past.
• Help them break down problems into manageable pieces
• Don't give generalized compliments. Make compliments specific.
• Put a problem or task in sequential order.
• Don't brainstorm. When they are in the grip of extraverted intuition, this will only make things worse.
• Let them engage their auxiliary extraverted feeling by reading materials that are personally moving or spiritual.
• Encourage them to get some physical exercise (without making it sound like an insult).
• Let them talk about their irrational fears or feelings, and give them quiet, calm reassurance.
• Take them seriously. Don't patronize or judge them.

ESFJ—THE CAREGIVER

What stresses out an ESFJ:

• Unstructured environments
• Having to do things that involve abstract, theoretical concepts
• Environments that have tension or conflict
• Unexpected change
• Inadequate time to complete work to their standards
• Tense or confrontational relationships or situations
• Situations that don't meld with their values
• Lack of trust in someone or something they're involved with
• Criticism
• Feeling unappreciated

When faced with stress, ESFJs can become very critical and overly sensitive, often imagining bad intentions where there aren't any. Being prone to insecurity, they can focus all their attention on pleasing those who give them security. This may lead them to become staunchly attached to a toxic relationship, structure, or belief system that provides them some sort of affirmation or security. They can become quite dramatic when under stress, finding fault with almost everyone and everything. They can experience low energy, a feeling of depression, and pessimism. They become uncharacteristically quiet and withdrawn. If they are under chronic stress, they may fall into the grip of their inferior function and introverted thinking. This can cause them to take on the form of "the condemner," focusing on everyone's flaws and all the ways they have been hurt by them and how those flaws go against their belief system and how things "should be."

How to help an ESFJ experiencing stress:

- Give them a change of scenery. Let them spend some time outdoors.
- Encourage them to exercise (without making it a dig at their weight or health).
- Watch a comedy with them, or engage them with some humor or light-hearted entertainment.
- Acknowledge how they feel.
- Let them talk it out.
- Remind them of their strengths and contributions.
- Don't use logic to talk them out of stress.
- Don't ignore them.
- Give them feedback. Talk about a similar situation you went through.
- Get them away from the environment or situation that is stressing them out.
- Give them an enjoyable book to read, or a lighthearted movie to watch.

ESTP—THE PROMOTER

What stresses out an ESTP:

- Rigidly enforced rules
- Having to plan far into the future
- Feeling out of control
- Being asked to complete tasks without detailed directions or processes
- Large amounts of book work, theory, or writing
- Being forced to make commitments or plans before they're ready
- Being forced to make decisions or eliminate options before they're ready
- Having to spend a lot of time following someone else's rules or schedule
- Being in a situation where they have to use a lot of theoretical or intuitive concepts
- Being around people who are excessively serious

When faced with stress, ESTPs tend to feel empty or hollow inside. Their first impulse may be to seek revenge for whatever has caused them stress.

They may do this by mocking other people's values or becoming increasingly antisocial and disdainful of others. If they are in a state of chronic stress, they may fall into the grip of their inferior function and introverted intuition, and become a "dramatizer." When this happens, they may do things that are completely out of character for them. They may lose their naturally easygoing, agreeable character and begin to have fearful fantasies of the future, ideas of impending doom swirling in their minds. They may begin to assign big meaning to small occurrences and become preoccupied with the meaning of life and the future of mankind and the universe in a way that is usually filled with gloom and disillusionment.

How to help an ESTP who is experiencing stress:

- Give them space initially or directly after the event.
- Listen to them. Understand that they will likely be irrational.
- Don't tell them how to fix it. This will only make them feel more helpless.
- Give gentle affirmations or encouragement
- Help them sort out their priorities, paying careful attention to their feelings.

ISTP—THE MECHANIC

What stresses out an ISTP:

- Tight restrictions and a rigid structure
- Being in controlling relationships
- Dealing with irrational people
- Having to use theoretical or intuitive concepts for a prolonged period
- Being in an emotionally charged environment
- Lack of alone time. Too much extraverting
- Being in a non-challenging work environment
- Doing repetitive, mundane tasks
- Not having their personal values respected or validated

When ISTPs experience an overload of stress, they may try to respond by lashing out against whatever is causing it. They may violate rules and regulations that they feel are controlling them; they may feel a need to "get even." They may become emotionally obsessed with logic and proving a point, while losing track of organization and losing objects or misplacing them. In cases of chronic stress, ISTPs may fall into the grip of their inferior function and extraverted feeling, and become very emotive. They will become hypersensitive about their relationships with others and misinterpret small, insignificant details into the belief that others dislike or hate them. They may become uncharacteristically emotional and bitter toward others.

How to help an ISTP experiencing stress:

- Give them alone time and space.
- Excuse them from some of their responsibilities.
- Let them "get away" from everything.
- Don't ask how they feel.
- Encourage them to exercise.
- Let them read a mystery novel or do something that engages light problem solving.
- Forgive their out-of-character behavior.

ISFP—THE ARTIST

What stresses out an ISFP:

- Rigid structure and rules
- Having to violate their deeply held values
- Not enough alone time; too much extraverting
- Too many demands or obligations
- Having to deal with excessive data
- Long-term planning
- Criticism
- Lack of appreciation from others
- Feeling that they are about to lose something (relationship/task, etc.)

When under stress, ISFPs can often become passive, aggressive, restless, and defiant. If stress continues to build, ISFPs may become self-destructive and careless of their own well-being in an effort to restore excitement or affirmation in their life. If ISFPs are in a state of chronic stress, they may fall into the grip of their inferior function and extraverted thinking, and become "the criticizer." They may be harsh and critical of others, obsessing over their mistakes and others' incompetence. They may have an intense urge to fix perceived problems or right wrongs, but this can often worsen the situation.

How to help an ISFP experiencing stress:

- Give them some time alone to process their feelings and thoughts.
- Validate their feelings, and listen to them. Female ISFPs are often ready to talk sooner about their feelings than male ISFPs.

- Remind them of their strengths.
- Don't give them advice. It won't help when they're stressed.
- Don't try to reason with them or be logical. Just be patient, calm, and affirming.
- Only after they've calmed down from the stress, ask if they'd like any help with solutions.

ESFP—THE PERFORMER

What stresses out an ESFP:

- An environment of rigidly enforced rules
- Long-term planning
- Having to think far into the future
- Being forced to make commitments and plans
- Criticism or confrontation
- Feeling out of control
- Being asked to complete tasks without detailed directions or processes
- Lack of hands-on experiences
- Too much time alone
- Too much book work, theory, or writing
- Having to sit still for too long

When ESFPs experience stress, they may become passively resistant initially. They might become bored and feel empty and listless. They may try to retaliate against the people who are causing them stress by annoying them or trying to irritate them. When overwhelmed with stress, they may become self-destructive, regressing emotionally, and acting in an immature fashion. In the case of chronic stress, ESFPs may fall into the grip of their inferior function and introverted intuition. When this happens, the ESFP can become highly exaggerative, dramatically foretelling the doom that the future will hold. They may see hidden meanings and visions of despair for the future, and struggle with misinterpreting things people say. This is highly uncharacteristic for an ESFP, since they are usually very optimistic and friendly people who want to maintain harmony.

How to help an ESFP experiencing stress:

- Listen thoughtfully and patiently.
- Give them space initially to sort out their feelings, but be ready to talk to them as ESFPs are often helped by talking things through.

- Understand that they will be irrational. Be patient with this.
- Don't tell them how to fix it. This makes them feel more helpless.
- Encourage them to exercise or spend some time outdoors.
- Tell them what they are doing well.

INFP—THE HEALER

What stresses out an INFP:

- Rigidity in rules and timelines
- Having values violated
- Not enough time alone; too much extraverting
- Too many demands on their time
- Small talk
- A lack of authenticity from others
- Having their creativity stifled
- Having to focus too extensively on sensory/concrete details
- Criticism or confrontation
- Fear that they might lose someone or something (relationship/task, etc.)

When under stress, INFPs get lost in internal turmoil. They feel caught between pleasing others and maintaining their own integrity and taking care of their well-being. Their natural tendency to identify with others, compounded with their self-sacrificial tendencies, leaves them confused about who they really are. They feel lost and perplexed during stressful times; and as stress builds they can fall into the grip of their inferior function and extraverted thinking. When this happens, they will do things that are typically out of character. They may become obsessed with fixing perceived problems and righting wrongs. They may blurt out hostile thoughts or engage in destructive fantasies directed at just about anyone available. They also may have biting sarcasm and cynicism. They may become aggressively critical to others and themselves, dwelling on all the "facts" necessary to support their overwhelming sense of failure.

How to help an INFP experiencing stress:

- Give them space and time alone to sort out their feelings.
- Validate their feelings.
- Remind them of their strengths.
- Don't give them advice. This will only make them feel worse.
- Let them "get away" from it all.

- Exercise can help. However, with these types it's best not to suggest it when they are stressed, but after, as a solution.
- Forgive them if they've been overly critical while stressed.
- Let them work on a project they've been interested in, but maybe have been too busy to spend time on.

ENFP—THE INSPIRER

What stresses out an ENFP:

- Environments where rules are rigidly enforced
- Focusing on repetitive, detailed tasks
- Having to focus too much on sensory details
- Having to focus too much on the past or present
- Not being able to use their intuition
- Constraints on brainstorming or envisioning
- A lack of outside stimulation
- Being micromanaged
- Having creativity stifled
- Having to complete projects before they're ready
- Criticism
- Lack of appreciation
- Having their values violated
- Overextending themselves for others

ENFPs tend to overextend themselves and procrastinate, which is often a source of stress as it complicates their lives. When they become stressed, their naturally charming natures become more irritable and oversensitive. When stressed, ENFPs feel alienated and engage in deceptions to obscure what is occurring within themselves. They will feel that they are losing control over their own independent identities and feel conflicted by intruding circumstances. During continued stress, they may fall into the grip of their inferior function and introverted sensing. When this happens, they become obsessive and depressed. They will become hyper-aware of minor bodily sensations or abnormalities and interpret them as a sign of a serious illness. They may have a hard time communicating clearly, and feel numb and frozen inside. Their thinking may become cloudy and convoluted. They will feel that there are no possibilities or ways out. They may feel overwhelmed, out of control, unable to sort out priorities, and thus become inflexible. Some become obsessive about recordkeeping, cleaning, or other household tasks.

How to help an ENFP with stress:

• Give them space and time alone to sort out their feelings.
• Remind them that they are able and competent.
• Give them permission to "escape."
• Don't give them advice. It won't help right now.
• Don't ask for details.
• Don't try to "fix" the problem.
• Meditation often helps them.
• Listen to them.
• Encourage them to exercise.
• Encourage them to get enough sleep.
• Encourage them to get a massage.
• Be warm and kind in the way you speak to them.
• After they've calmed down a little, ask them if they want help evaluating the situation.

INFJ—THE COUNSELOR

What stresses out an INFJ:

• Having to focus too much on sensory/concrete details
• An overload of sensory stimulation or noise
• Interruptions
• Distress within a close relationship
• Having their values violated
• Not enough alone time; too much extraverting
• Working with closed-minded people
• Lack of appreciation or understanding
• Unfamiliar environments with overwhelming amounts of details
• Having plans disrupted
• Not having a clear direction
• Lack of harmony
• Criticism and conflict
• Not being able to use their intuition or envision the future
• Having to focus too much on the present

When under stress, INFJs feel fragmented or lost. They feel like they can't be themselves and feel an urge to act a part to "survive" or fit in. This disassociation can cause physical symptoms for the INFJ, like headaches, IBS, or nausea. The repressed feelings they're holding on to can cause them to become immobilized. If they are under chronic extreme stress, they may fall into the grip of their inferior function and extraverted sensing. When this happens, they may engage in indulgent, self-destructive habits like binge-eating, watching too much television, over-exercising, or drinking too much. This often feels like an out-of-body experience to them. What they do provides no pleasure, but feels somewhat robotic and out of control. After this occurs, they dwell in self-hatred, falling even more into guilt over what they've done. They may become uncharacteristically angry and quick-tempered, unreasonable, and irrational. They may become obsessed with details in their outer world, obsessively cleaning or doing housework. They stumble over their words, and their intense feelings may eventually lead them to a state of complete exhaustion.

How to help an INFJ experiencing stress:

- Give them space.
- Reduce sensory stimulation, music, interruptions, TV, etc.
- Let them express their thoughts and feelings.
- Understand that they may be irrational. Don't judge them.
- Don't give advice. This will only stress them out further.
- Let them take a break from some of their responsibilities.
- Encourage them to spend some time in nature, walking, or reading a book.
- Take a walk with them if they want company.
- Encourage their less serious side, and let them relieve emotional tension by letting them cry through a sappy movie or novel of some sort.
- Be forgiving if they've been overly harsh or critical while under stress. Chances are they will feel very guilty about it.

Related: The childhood struggles of INFJs.

ENFJ—THE GIVER

What stresses out an ENFJ:

- Being in critical or confrontational environments
- Lack of appreciation or affirmation
- Lack of harmony
- Unexpected change
- Inadequate time to complete work to their standards
- Tense relationships or environments
- Having to do mundane, repetitive tasks

- Having to conform with something that goes against their values
- Overempathizing with others to the point of losing track of their own needs
- Being misunderstood or not trusted
- People not living up to their idealized expectations

When ENFJs experience stress, they often disassociate themselves from the situation in an effort to protect their sense of well-being and togetherness. They may repress the unpleasant side of life for so long that it gradually intensifies until the ENFJ explodes with emotion and charged anger. Often the ENFJ's body will reflect pent-up stress by manifesting various physical symptoms, like headaches, shoulder tension, or an upset stomach. In the case of chronic stress, the ENFJ may fall into the grip of their inferior function and introverted thinking. When this happens, the ENFJ may uncharacteristically lash out at others and obsess over their mistakes, lack of competence, and flaws. Eventually, these criticisms will turn inward, and the ENFJ will withdraw from others to self-criticize. She may become obsessive about analyzing irrelevant data to find some ultimate truth or reason for her stress.

How to help an ENFJ experiencing stress:

- Acknowledge how they feel.
- Let them talk it out.
- Remind them of their strengths and contributions.
- Don't use logic to talk them out of their stress.
- Don't ignore them, even if they seem irrational.
- Give them a change of scenery to get away from the situation.
- Go outdoors. Do some type of exercise with them.
- Watch a lighthearted movie or comedy with them.
- Do not patronize or dismiss their concerns.

INTJ—THE MASTERMIND

What stresses out an INTJ:

- Being in an environment that doesn't appreciate their skills, visions, or ideas
- Not enough alone time; too much extraverting
- Too much noise or sensory input
- Working with those they see as lazy, incompetent, or ignorant
- Having to pay attention to too many details at once
- Being in unfamiliar environments

- Having their well-settled plans disrupted
- Too much focus on the here and now
- Not being able to use their intuition to envision the future

When in a state of stress, the INTJ can feel an immense amount of pressure—as if everything is on the line. To an INTJ, this often means the ability to produce something significant is somehow stifled. They may find themselves overwhelmed, thinking about ideas and options that don't have a productive end. As stress increases, the INTJ can become argumentative and disagreeable. Social interaction becomes increasingly difficult; and they may become preoccupied with obsessive ideas and plans. They may start to spend a massive amount of time fighting horrible thoughts and feelings of worthlessness. They will ruminate about their mistakes, inadequacies, and weaknesses, and stop progress on a project for fear of failure. In a case of chronic stress, the INTJ may fall into the grip of their inferior function and extraverted sensing. When this happens, they may give into self-destructive indulgences, like overeating, over-exercising, over-drinking, or buying lots of useless items. They may obsessively clean or reorganize files.

How to help an INTJ experiencing stress:

- Give them space and time alone to process their thoughts and feelings.
- Reduce sensory stimulation like noise, TV, radio, or bright lights.
- Let them express their thoughts and feelings without judgment. Understand that they may be irrational.
- Don't give them advice. This will only make them feel worse.
- Give them a break from responsibilities.
- Encourage them to get enough sleep at night.
- Help them lighten their schedule or cancel unnecessary activities.
- After some time of solitude, encourage them to get a change of scenery by going outdoors.

ENTJ—THE EXECUTIVE

What stresses out an ENTJ:

- Being in an environment that lacks vision or ideas for the future
- Being in an environment where others don't appreciate their vision
- Being interrupted
- Being surrounded by (or guilty of) incompetence
- Poorly managed change

- Laziness
- Having to be a follower instead of a leader
- Not being able to make their goals come to fruition
- Having to deal with intense emotions from others
- Feeling guilt over being critical toward others
- Not having their strongly held values validated or respected
- Small talk or frivolous conversations

When experiencing stress, ENTJs may at first become argumentative and combative with anyone who is causing it. They may feel that they are losing control and feel an urgent need to complete a task. If the stress continues, they become distracted by the urgency and need to get something done. They may engage in compulsive, misdirected activities like cleaning, counting, or inspecting. They will feel a growing sense of failure, and a rising sense of anger and frustration. If they are in a state of chronic stress, they may fall into the grip of their inferior function and introverted feeling. When this happens, they may become uncharacteristically emotional and furious and withdraw from others to prevent anyone seeing their lack of emotional stability. They may become hypersensitive about their relationships, misinterpreting tiny, insignificant details and believing that others hate or dislike them.

How to help an ENTJ experiencing stress:

- Give them some space and time alone to sort out their feelings.
- Listen and let them talk it out when they're ready.
- Discuss information or ideas that could lead to solutions.
- Don't be overly sympathetic or emotional.
- Give them a change of scenery by getting outdoors with them.
- Encourage them to vent their frustration without fear of judgment.
- Remind them that they are OK, and it is perfectly fine to feel the way they do and that you won't judge them.

INTP—THE THINKER

What stresses out an INTP:

- Being in an environment where they feel controlled by others
- Not being allowed to go with the flow of the moment
- Being required to do simple and repetitive tasks
- Being surrounded by individuals they see as incompetent
- A lack of autonomy

- Being in charge of the quality of another person's work
- Not enough alone time; too much extraverting
- Being immersed in emotionally charged environments
- Being in a place where their expertise is not appreciated
- People "barging in" on their space
- Not having their strongly held values validated

When INTPs begin to experience stress, they often feel highly self-critical and powerless. If stress continues, they feel as if their mind is blocked and they can't access all the vital information they've stored there. Their creativity comes to a halt, and they may suffer from stage fright, writer's block, and a general inhibition of their usual ingenious thinking. The INTP may become self-conscious and distracted in anticipation of failure. If they become too overwhelmed with stress, they may stop taking any risks and fail to gain the expertise and mastery they need. In the case of chronic stress, the INTP may fall into the grip of their inferior function and extroverted feeling. This may cause them to have uncharacteristic emotional outbursts and become edgy, illogical, inefficient, and obsessed with details.

How to help an INTP experiencing stress:

- Give them alone time and space.
- Excuse them from some of their responsibilities.
- Let them get away from everything.
- Don't ask them how they feel or if they're OK.
- Encourage them to have some alone time exercising.
- Let them know it's OK to feel unreasonable sometimes.
- Stay out of the way and forgive out-of-characteristic behavior.

ENTP—THE INVENTOR

What stresses out an ENTP:

- An environment where rules are rigidly enforced
- A lack of change or progression
- A lack of outside stimulation
- Being micromanaged
- Having their creativity stifled
- Being forced to make decisions or complete projects before they're ready
- Working with individuals they view as incompetent
- Not having their visions appreciated

- Having their principles violated
- Having to focus too long on mundane details
- Overextending themselves

When ENTPs are experiencing stress, they become distracted and overwhelmed, losing their signature "can-do" attitude. They may feel incompetent, inept, and inadequate. They can become overwhelmed with fear, panic, and anxiety, and will feel a need to escape whatever situation is plaguing them. Their creativity will be stifled, and if the stress isn't handled, they will fall into the grip of their inferior function and introverted sensing. When they fall into the grip of their inferior function, they will become uncharacteristically quiet and reserved. They will feel depressed and stew on ways they have failed. They may notice minor bodily changes and become convinced that they are suffering from some life-threatening disease. They often become hypochondriacs, imagining all kinds of ailments that are befalling them physically.

How to help an ENTP experiencing stress:

- Give them time alone to deal with their feelings.
- Avoid patronizing them, even if they are being irrational.
- Don't try to "solve the problem."
- Listen without making judgments, or trying to talk them out of their negative state.
- Encourage them to have some time alone to exercise.
- Encourage them to get enough rest.
- Give them a massage.
- After they've calmed down a little, ask if they want help.

Appendix B: Jungian Types

ISTJ

Quiet, serious, earn success by thoroughness and dependability. Practical, matter-of-fact, realistic, and responsible. Decide logically what should be done and work toward it steadily, regardless of distractions. Take pleasure in making everything orderly and organized—their work, their home, their life. Value traditions and loyalty.

ISFJ

Quiet, friendly, responsible, and conscientious. Committed and steady in meeting their obligations. Thorough, painstaking, and accurate. Loyal, considerate, notice and remember specifics about people who are important to them, concerned with how others feel. Strive to create an orderly and harmonious environment at work and at home.

INFJ

Seek meaning and connection in ideas, relationships, and material possessions. Want to understand what motivates people and are insightful about others. Conscientious and committed to their firm values. Develop a clear vision about how best to serve the common good. Organized and decisive in implementing their vision.

INTJ

Have original minds and great drive for implementing their ideas and achieving their goals. Quickly see patterns in external events and develop long-range explanatory perspectives. When committed, organize a job and carry it through. Skeptical and independent, have high standards of competence and performance—for themselves and others.

ISTP

Tolerant and flexible, quiet observers until a problem appears, then act quickly to find workable solutions. Analyze what makes things work and readily get through large amounts of data to isolate the core of practical problems. Interested in cause and effect, organize facts using logical principles, value efficiency.

ISFP

Quiet, friendly, sensitive, and kind. Enjoy the present moment, what's going on around them. Like to have their own space and to work within their own time frame. Loyal and committed to their values and to people who are important to them. Dislike disagreements and conflicts, do not force their opinions or values on others.

INFP

Idealistic, loyal to their values and to people who are important to them. Want an external life that is congruent with their values. Curious, quick to see possibilities, can be catalysts for implementing ideas. Seek to understand people and to help them fulfill their potential. Adaptable, flexible, and accepting unless a value is threatened.

INTP

Seek to develop logical explanations for everything that interests them. Theoretical and abstract, interested more in ideas than in social interaction. Quiet, contained, flexible, and adaptable. Have unusual ability to focus in depth to solve problems in their area of interest. Skeptical, sometimes critical, always analytical.

ESTP

Flexible and tolerant, they take a pragmatic approach focused on immediate results. Theories and conceptual explanations bore them—they want to act energetically to solve the problem. Focus on the here-and-now, spontaneous, enjoy each moment that they can be active with others. Enjoy material comforts and style. Learn best through doing.

ESFP

Outgoing, friendly, and accepting. Exuberant lovers of life, people, and material comforts. Enjoy working with others to make things happen. Bring common sense and a realistic approach to their work, and make work fun. Flexible and spontaneous, adapt readily to new people and environments. Learn best by trying a new skill with other people.

ENFP

Warmly enthusiastic and imaginative. See life as full of possibilities. Make connections between events and information very quickly, and confidently proceed based on the patterns they see. Want a lot of affirmation from others, and readily give appreciation and support. Spontaneous and flexible, often rely on their ability to improvise and their verbal fluency.

ENTP

Quick, ingenious, stimulating, alert, and outspoken. Resourceful in solving new and challenging problems. Adept at generating conceptual possibilities and then analyzing them strategically. Good at reading other people. Bored by routine, will seldom do the same thing the same way, apt to turn to one new interest after another.

ESTJ

Practical, realistic, matter-of-fact. Decisive, quickly move to implement decisions. Organize projects and people to get things done, focus on getting results in the most efficient way possible. Take care of routine details. Have a clear set of logical standards, systematically follow them and want others to also. Forceful in implementing their plans.

ESFJ

Warmhearted, conscientious, and cooperative. Want harmony in their environment, work with determination to establish it. Like to work with others to complete tasks accurately and on time. Loyal, follow through even in small matters. Notice what others need in their day-by-day lives and try to provide it. Want to be appreciated for who they are and for what they contribute.

ENFJ

Warm, empathetic, responsive, and responsible. Highly attuned to the emotions, needs, and motivations of others. Find potential in everyone, want to help others fulfill their potential. May act as catalysts for individual and group growth. Loyal, responsive to praise and criticism. Sociable, facilitate others in a group, and provide inspiring leadership.

ENTJ

Frank, decisive, assume leadership readily. Quickly see illogical and inefficient procedures and policies, develop and implement comprehensive systems to solve organizational problems. Enjoy long-term planning and goal setting. Usually well informed, well read, enjoy expanding their knowledge and passing it on to others. Forceful in presenting their ideas.

Source: Excerpted from *Introduction to Type*, by Isabel Briggs Myers, published by CPP, Inc. Used with permission.

Appendix C: Characteristics Frequently Associated with Each of the Myers-Briggs Psychological Types

Source: Myers & McCaulley, *Manual: A Guide to the Development and Use of the Myers-Briggs Type Indicator.*

ISTJ

Serious, quiet, earn success by concentration and thoroughness. Practical, orderly, matter-of-fact, logical, realistic, and dependable. See to it that everything is well organized. Take responsibility. Make up their own minds as to what should be accomplished and work toward it steadily, regardless of protests or distractions.

ISFJ

Quiet, friendly, responsible, and conscientious. Work devotedly lo meet their obligations. Lend stability to any project or group. Thorough, painstaking, accurate. Their interests are usually not technical. Can be patient with necessary details. Loyal, considerate, perceptive, concerned with how other people feel.

INFJ

Succeed by perseverance, originality, and desire to do whatever is needed or wanted. Put their best efforts into their work. Quietly forceful, conscientious, concerned for others. Respected for their firm principles. Likely to be honored and followed for their clear convictions as to how best to serve the common good.

INTJ

Usually have original minds and great drive for their own ideas and purposes. In fields that appeal to them, they have a fine power to organize a job and carry it through with or without help. Skeptical, critical, independent, determined, sometimes stubborn. Must learn to yield less important points in order to win the most important.

ISTP

Cool onlookers, quiet, reserved, observing and analyzing life with detached curiosity and unexpected flashes of original humor. Usually interested in cause and effect. How and why mechanical things work, and in organizing facts using logical principles.

ISFP

Refiring, quietly friendly, sensitive, kind, modest about their abilities. Shun disagreements, do not force their opinions or values on others. Usually do not care to lead but are often loyal followers. Often relaxed about getting things done, because they enjoy the present moment and do not want to spoil by undue haste or exertion.

INFP

Full of enthusiasms and loyalties, but seldom talk of these until they know you well. Care about learning, ideas, language, and independent projects of their own. Tend to undertake too much, then somehow get it done. Friendly, but often too absorbed in what they are doing to be sociable. Little concerned with possessions or physical surroundings.

INTP

Quiet and reserved. Especially enjoy theoretical or scientific pursuits. Like solving problems with logic and analysis. Usually interested mainly in ideas, with little liking for parties or small talk. Tend to have sharply defined interests. Need careers where some strong interest can be used and useful.

ESTP

Good at on-the-spot problem solving. Do not worry, enjoy whatever comes along. Tend to like mechanical things and sports, with friends on the side. Adaptable, tolerant, generally conservative in values. Dislike long explanations. Are best with real things that can be worked, handled, taken apart, or put together.

ESFP

Outgoing, easygoing, accepting, friendly, enjoy everything and make things more fun for others by their enjoyment. Like sports and making things happen. Know what's going on and join in eagerly. Find remembering facts easier than mastering theories. Are best in situations that need sound common sense and practical ability with people as well as with things.

ENFP

Warmly enthusiastic, high-spirited, ingenious, imaginative. Able to do almost anything that interests them. Quick with a solution for any difficulty and ready to help anyone with a problem. Often rely on their ability to improvise instead of preparing in advance. Can usually find compelling reasons for whatever they want.

ENTP

Quick, ingenious, good at many things. Stimulating company, alert and outspoken. May argue for fun on either side of a question. Resourceful in solving new and challenging problems, but may neglect routine assignments. Apt to turn to one new interest after another. Skillful in finding logical reasons for what they want.

ESTJ

Practical, realistic, matter-of-fact, with a natural head for business of mechanics. Not interested in subjects they see no use for, but can apply themselves when necessary, Like to organize and run activities. May make good administrators, especially if they remember to consider others' feelings and points of view.

ESFJ

Warm-hearted, talkative, popular, conscientious, born cooperators, active committee members. Need harmony and may be good at creating it. Always doing something nice for someone. Work best with encouragement and praise. Main interest is in things that directly and visibly affect people's lives.

ENFJ

Responsive and responsible. Generally feel real concern for what others think or want, and try to handle things with due regard for the other person's feelings. Can present a proposal or lead a group discussion with ease and tact. Sociable, popular, sympathetic. Responsive to praise and criticism.

ENTJ

Hearty, frank, decisive, leaders in activities. Usually good in anything that requires reasoning and intelligent talk, such as public speaking. Are usually well informed and enjoy adding to their fund of knowledge. May sometimes appear more positive and confident than their experience in an area.

Index

About the Authors

Clifford Mayes, PhD, PsyD, received a doctorate in the history of U.S. education from the University of Utah and a doctorate in psychology from the Southern California University for Professional Studies. Until his retirement, he was a professor of education at Brigham Young University and is now an adjunct professor of psychology at Pacifica Graduate Institute in Carpinteria, California. Mayes has authored ten books and forty scholarly articles in psychology, educational psychology, curriculum theory, and multiculturalism.

Mark R. Grandstaff, PhD, has a dual degree in American history and institutional culture from the University of Wisconsin at Madison. Having written four books and over seventy articles, he has taught at Brigham Young University (emeritus associate professor), the University of California at Berkeley (associate professor), and the University of Maryland, University College. Dr. Grandstaff is currently a fellow of the James MacGregor Burns Institute of Strategic Leadership, College Park.

Alexandra Fidyk, PhD, serves as associate professor in the Department of Secondary Education, University of Alberta, and is associate editor of the *International Journal of Jungian Studies*. A past president of the *Jungian Society of Scholarly Studies* and now joint editor of *Poetic Inquiry: Enchantment of Place*, Fidyk is a certified Jungian psychotherapist; an integrated body psychotherapist; a constellation and family system therapist; and a lover of horses, cats, and nature.

Lightning Source UK Ltd.
Milton Keynes UK
UKHW011128271219
355975UK00001B/394/P